25 WALKS

THE
COTSWOLDS

N

WARWICK

Royal Leamington Spa

Worcester

Stratford on Avon

Avon

M40

HEREFORD AND WORCESTER

Evesham

23

24

25

Banbury

22

21

M50

Severn

16

15

18

19

Chipping Norton

13

20

Charlbury

Oxford

Cheltenham

17

Gloucester

Evenlode

GLOUCESTER

14

Windrush

8

11

7

Stroud

9

12

OXFORD

10

Cirencester

Thames

5

6

Didcot

Chipping Sodbury

Swindon

M4

Wootton Bassett

BERKSHIRE

4

M4

3

AVON

Chippenham

Marlborough

Kennet

Newbury

2

1

Devizes

Bath

Avon

Trowbridge

WILTSHIRE

Frome

Warminster

Andover

HAMPSHIRE

Test

M3

Salisbury

Avon

25 WALKS

THE COTSWOLDS

Ted Fryer

Series Editor: Roger Smith

EDINBURGH:THE STATIONERY OFFICE

First published 1996

Applications for reproduction should be made to The Stationery Office.

Acknowledgements

Many people contribute to a book which apparently has only one author. I have
learnt so much from them over the years. Cotswold Wardens, the Cotswold
Countryside Service and the Rights of Way officers of six county councils, 14
district councils and the Countryside Commission have given me the opportunity
to range over the Cotswolds and meet many residents, farmers and others with
deep local knowledge, as well as help open up and maintain rights of way for us all
to enjoy.
In addition, I would like to thank Mrs Daphne Ransome of the Gloucestershire
Federation of Women's Institutes, and Mrs Rosemary Hancock (Phoenix
Bookshop, Winchcombe) who gave me a lift when the bus timetable had
changed.
Most of the photographs are my own but I have raided the collections of
Gloucestershire County Council for some of the pictures. I found a gold mine of
photographs in Bill Potter's collection and my thanks go to him for his generosity
in letting me use them.
My special thanks go to my wife Judy, not only for constructive criticism, but also
for keeping the home front going while I went off and enjoyed myself.
Thanks are due to the Bugatti Museum for their kind permission to reproduce the
photograph on page 61.

British Library Cataloguing in Publication Data

A catalogue record for this book is available from the British Library

ISBN 0 11 495726 6

CONTENTS

USEFUL INFORMATION

The length of each walk is given in kilometres and miles, but within the text measurements are metric for simplicity. In some walks, a shorter alternative is offered; the distances for each are given. The approximate amount of time you should allow for each walk is also given. It is based on a walking speed of two miles per hour (3.2km), but it does not include allowances for stops for lunch, cream teas, or visits to attractions.

The walks are described in detail and are supported by maps. Between text and map, you should not get lost, but if you want a back-up, the Ordnance Survey 1:25,000 Pathfinder maps show field boundaries and rights of way. They are on sale locally.

Please park considerately, in such a way that you will not hinder either other visitors or local people while you are away. If you intend to visit an inn, ask the landlord if you can leave your car there during closing hours. Where feasible, information is included about reaching start points by public transport. Timetables can be obtained from Tourist Information Centres.

If you find a path obstructed, you may divert from it in a reasonable manner. You must not cause damage, and you must not leave a dangerous situation, for example, leaving a gate open so that livestock could escape. By law, a cross-field path should be restored after ploughing (within 14 days) or other cultivation (24 hours). If it has not been restored, you still have the right to walk through the crop on the line of the right of way.

Every care has been taken to make the descriptions and maps as accurate as possible, but the author and publishers can accept no responsibility for errors, however caused. The countryside is always changing and there will inevitably be alterations to some aspects of these walks as time goes by. The author and publishers would be happy to receive comments and suggested alterations for future editions of the book.

METRIC MEASUREMENTS

At the beginning of each walk, the distance is given in miles and kilometres. Within the text, all measurements are metric for simplicity (and indeed our Ordnance Survey maps are now all metric). However, it was felt that a conversion table might be useful to those readers who, like the author, still tend to think in Imperial terms.

The basic statistic to remember is that one kilometre is five-eighths of a mile. Half a mile is equivalent to 800 metres and a quarter-mile is 400 metres. Below that distance, yards and metres are little different in practical terms.

km	miles
1	0.625
1.6	1
2	1.25
3	1.875
3.2	2
4	2.5
4.8	3
5	3.125
6	3.75
6.4	4
7	4.375
8	5
9	5.625
10	6.25
16	10

INTRODUCTION

A full 5000 years of history in the Cotswolds means that you can expect Iron Age hill forts, Roman roads, medieval monasteries, grand mansionhouses, and much else besides. Cotswold 'vernacular' architecture is a satisfying style developed centuries ago in sympathy with the Jurassic oolite limestone, laid down in warm seas 150 million years ago. The rock strata were later heaved up in the west to form a scarp overlooking the Severn valley, and sloping gently eastwards towards the Thames.

The Cotswolds Area of Outstanding Natural Beauty (AONB) covers about 800 square miles (3000 sq km) in six counties. It is mostly farmland, cultivated and pasture, and woodland. It is important therefore to keep to rights of way, to avoid trespass and difficulty for those who manage the land as farmers and foresters.

The authorities have done much to open, clear and sign footpaths and bridleways, through their Rights of Way staff, ably assisted by many dedicated volunteers. Cotswold Voluntary Wardens (part of the Cotswold Countryside Service) contribute the equivalent of 22 fulltime staff in a year.

Many other volunteers help in different ways through parish councils, British Trust for Conservation Volunteers, Ramblers' Association and clubs. Many landowners and farmers also help effectively as volunteers.

The routes in this guide all follow public rights of way. You may find over time some alterations to the routes described. Farmers remove fences, or put up new ones; waymarks disappear; woodland gets felled. Sometimes local practice deviates from the Definitive Map for convenience, or a path may be legally diverted. Changes should be waymarked: please follow the new waymarked route.

The walks are suitable for families. Length ranges from 4 km (2 miles) to 13 km (8 miles), with most in the 8–10 km (5–6 miles) range. Even the longest (from Tetbury) is easy farmland and parkland walking with little climbing involved.

I always wear boots and trousers because I always seem to find mud and nettles! Others find trainers and shorts quite sufficient, in summer at least. However, do not underestimate the Cotswolds. Go well prepared, particularly in bad weather. Remember it is often a layer or two colder higher up.

Please keep dogs under strict control. A farmer is happier if he sees your dog on a lead. Remember he has powers to shoot any dog seen harassing livestock. Please also ensure your children respect the property they are crossing, and the herds and flocks you walk through. Enjoy the wild flowers, but please do not pick them: leave them for others to enjoy after you.

I hope you will enjoy following these walks as much as I have enjoyed describing them, and that they will whet your appetite to find out more about this lovely area.

TED FRYER

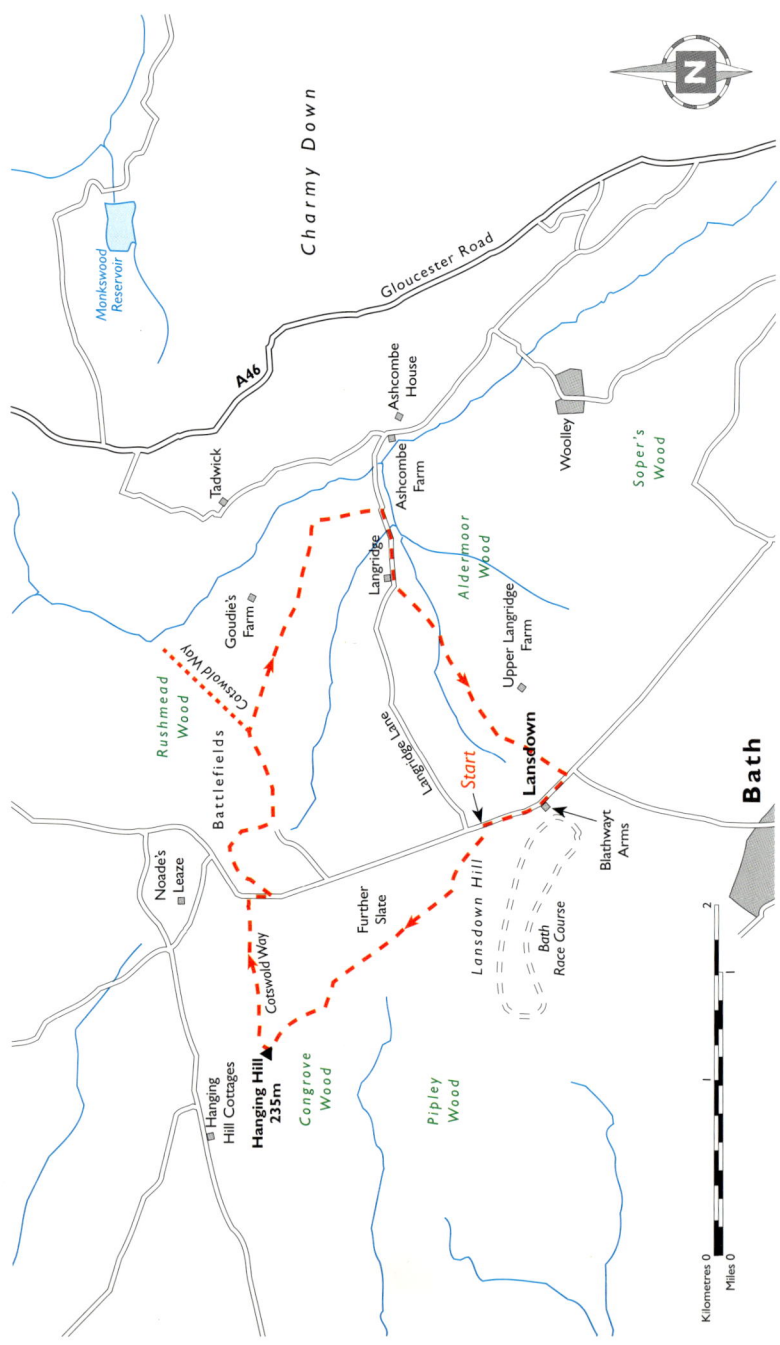

Charmy Down

Gloucester Road

A46

Monkswood Reservoir

Tadwick

Ashcombe House

Ashcombe Farm

Woolley

Soper's Wood

Langridge

Aldermoor Wood

Upper Langridge Farm

Goudie's Farm

Rushmead Wood

Cotswold Way

Battlefields

Lansdown

Start

Langridge Lane

Blathwayt Arms

Bath

Noade's Leaze

Further Slate

Lansdown Hill

Bath Race Course

Cotswold Way

Hanging Hill 235m

Hanging Hill Cottages

Congrove Wood

Pipley Wood

Kilometres 0

Miles 0

LANSDOWN

L ansdown hosts several recreational facilities for Bath – sports playing fields, golf course and racecourse; more peaceable competition than on the day in July 1643 when Cavaliers and Roundheads clashed here.

From the parking place, cross the major road, and a few metres to the left, enter the racecourse access road. Follow the road to the right. Before entering the parking area and the golf course, turn right on a track with a field wall on the right and the golf course on the left. At the next junction, continue ahead, beside the right-hand woodland. Cross another track and at the end of the woodland, bear left on the descending track to a gate.

Before the gate, climb the bank on the right, to follow the Cotswold Way over a wooden stile. Keep beside the wall on the left and enjoy fine views over the valley of the River Avon as it winds its way from Saltford on the left through Keynsham, past the large red buildings of the former Fry's chocolate factory, and into Bristol. Binoculars will help you pick out the Clifton Suspension Bridge.

At the Ordnance Survey pillar on the 'nose' of Hanging Hill, the view opens out up the Severn Vale. North of Bristol, the Severn Bridge crosses the river, with the Forest of Dean beyond it on the far bank. Gloucestershire's May Hill with its distinctive clump of trees is followed on the right by the scarp of Stinchcombe Hill. To the right again, the skyline is broken by the Tyndale Monument (Walk 5), with the southern Cotswold scarp seen edge-on. The nearest hill is Freezing Hill.

Cross the stile beyond the trig pillar and turn sharp right to follow the fence to a wall and into Beach Wood beside the fire brigade centre with its radio mast. At the lane, bear right and follow the drive from the fire brigade centre. It bears right with the

INFORMATION

Distance: 8 km (5 miles).

Start and finish: Parking place close to bus stop at Langridge turn, opposite Bath Racecourse. This is 3 km north-west of Bath city centre on the Bath, Lansdown/ Racecourse, Wick road.

Terrain: Easy walking with a gentle climb towards the end. No special footwear needed.

Time: Allow 3-4 hours.

Public transport: Badgerline from Bath to Ensleigh, 2 km south of start. Walk along road and join walk near the end. Bus stop at parking place is served infrequently but is possible.

Refreshments: Blathwayt Arms, 500 m south of start and passed just before the end of the walk.

The Granville Monument on Lansdown. Killed at the Civil War Battle in 1643, Sir Bevil died at Cold Ashton rectory.

Cotswold Way, cutting across the new tree planting to the road. Cross over and follow the Cotswold Way over a stile to the Granville monument.

These fields saw the Civil War Battle of Lansdown in 1643. The Royalist Sir Bevil Granville, from Cornwall, led an attack from Freezing Hill. The Parliamentarian force quietly retreated to Bath, but the mortally wounded Sir Bevil was carried to Cold Ashton, where he died at the Manor (Walk 2). When at Sudeley Castle (Walk 16), King Charles I wrote a letter of thanks to the Cornishmen for their unswerving loyalty.

From the monument bear right into woodland, over a wall stile, and follow the left-hand boundary. There is a view over Battlefields House to Freezing Hill beyond. The path bears right into the field to follow the left-hand wall. Over another wall stile, bear left down the slope into a track which, after a gate, is enclosed. Where the Cotswold Way turns into a field on the left on its way north, keep on the track, bearing gently right downhill.

There are views over the farmsteads of the Hamswell valley, and vehicles on the A46 can be seen on the skyline. The hedges beside the track contain many species, which might give a clue to their age, according to the theory that in a 30 m length every species represents 100 years.

Freezing Hill from which Sir Bevel launched his assault.

Reaching a gate and a lane by farm buildings, turn right to reach another lane. Turn right again, walking up this lane to the church high on the right-hand bank above. It contains a lot of interest including a Norman dog-tooth arched porch door and a chancel arch. Tablets commemorate members of the Blathwayt family from Dyrham (Walk 4).

Continue up the lane from the church, passing Court Farm. Just beyond it, turn left to follow a footpath across the field. Upper Langridge Farm is on the hillside ahead. Continue into the next field, converging on the woodland at the far corner. Cross the brook, turning right over the bridge and ascending the field parallel to the right-hand hedge line to the top right corner. A view over Upper Langridge is on the

Langridge on its long ridge.

right, although Upper Langridge Farm is in the trees above to the left. The tranquillity of this valley contrasts with the bustling centre of Bath only 5 km (3 miles) away.

Into the next field, bear gently left up the slope. At a point where scattered stones indicate a long fallen wall, bear more sharply left up to a stone stile (concrete slab actually). Beyond, bear right on the farm drive to the road on Lansdown. Turn right and follow the right-hand verge, past the cottages on the right and the Blathwayt Arms on the left, to reach the start point.

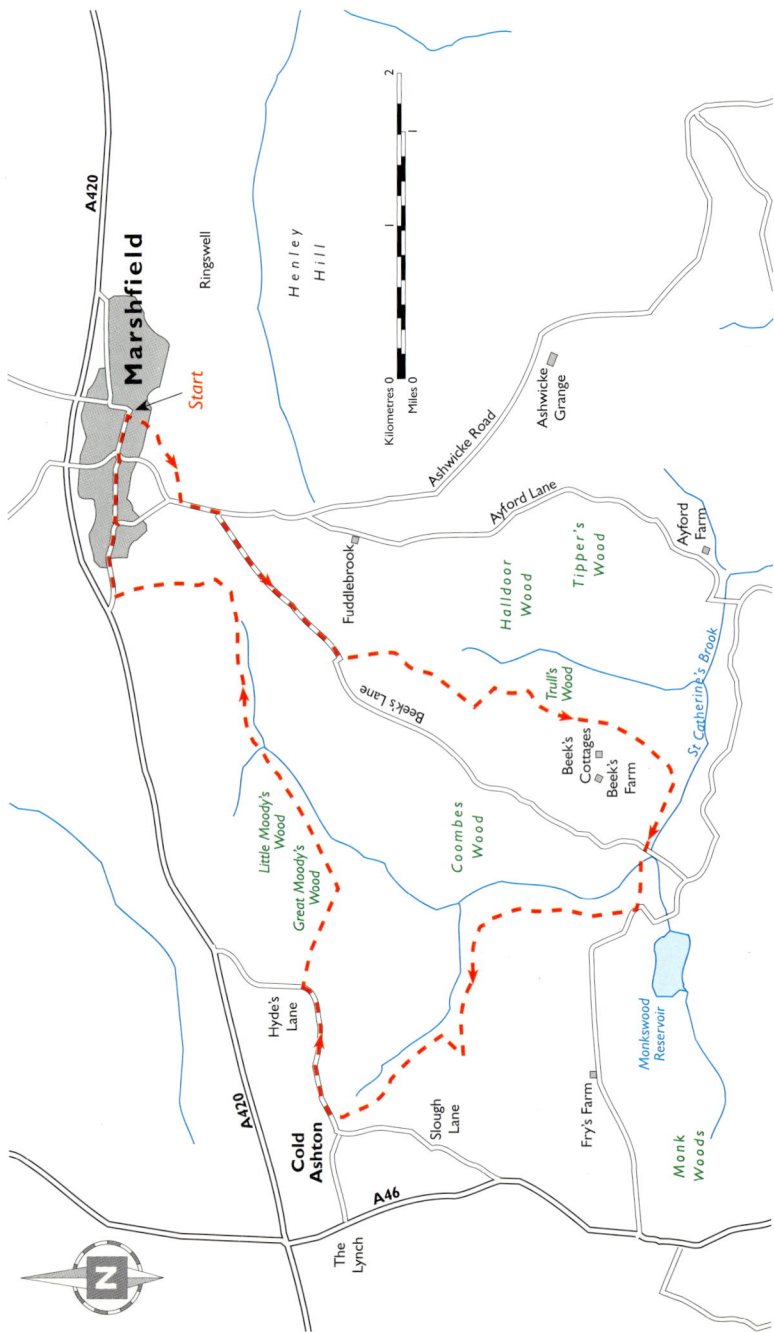

Marshfield

A420

Ringswell

Start

H e n l e y   H i l l

Kilometres 0
Miles 0

Ashwicke Road

Ashwicke
Grange

Ayford Lane

Fuddlebrook

Halldoor
Wood

Tipper's
Wood

Ayford
Farm

Beek's Lane

Trull's
Wood

St Catherine's Brook

Beek's
Cottages
Beek's
Farm

Little Moody's
Wood

Great Moody's
Wood

Coombes
Wood

Monkswood
Reservoir

Hyde's
Lane

Cold
Ashton

A420

Slough
Lane

Fry's Farm

Monk
Woods

A46

The
Lynch

N

MARSHFIELD

The village of Marshfield stands on the lip of a valley which formed the boundary of the ancient kingdoms of Wessex and Mercia. In 1996 it returned to Gloucestershire (from Avon), so the Three Shires Stone on the Fosseway to the south-east will once again be the meeting place of Gloucestershire, Wiltshire and Somerset.

Marshfield's stone buildings may seem rather forbidding in the rain; sunshine changes all that. The wealth of architecture arose from prosperity brought by the wool and malting trades. It is a lively village with its primary school, shops and other businesses and voluntary activities. The Marshfield Mummers, in costumes made from strips of newspaper, perform the revived version of their play on Boxing Day each year.

'103 miles from Hyde Park Corner' proclaims the plate on a wall near the Crown, showing the village's importance as a stage on the way from Bristol to London in coaching days.

From the bus shelter outside the school, opposite the Crown, walk down Weir Lane. Turn left beyond the farm buildings, go through a kissing gate and bear right diagonally down and up the field to a stile, a little to the left of the far right-hand corner. Turn right on the track and left at the road. Bear right down Beek's Lane, and pass Knowle Hill Farm on the left. As the road begins to descend the view ahead is towards Lansdown (Walk 1).

Turn left at a bridleway sign (Halldoor Lane). Where the lane 'kinks', turn right over a stile, following the upper right-hand edge of the steep field, continuing to another stile. A waymarked legal diversion, to avoid farm buildings further on, is an improvement for both walker and farmer.

Cross the stile, turn left down the field and right at the field corner. Over the next stile,

Marshfield was on the 18th and 19th century coaching route from London to Bristol.

103 MILES FROM HYDE PARK CORNER

ORIGINAL REMOVED DURING 1939–45 WAR

follow the left-hand headland on the edge of the ridge, with good views down the St Catherine's valley towards Bath. This route lies in the valley stretching to the right. Cross the lane to the stile opposite. Bear

Sheep safely grazing outside Cold Ashton Manor, looking over the St. Catherine's valley.

diagonally right across the field to another stile. Monkswood reservoir is in the valley, looking half right. Descend the steep slope beyond, to the right of the trees and bushes marking a rising spring. Continue down to cross a stile/footbridge/stile in the right-hand hedge, thus joining the Limestone Link footpath, which runs from the Mendips to the Cotswolds.

Keeping parallel to St Catherine's Brook on the left, cross two fields (passing a waymark post for this end of the diverted path) to leave by a stile and into the drive of the house on the right.

Cross the drive and the next stile, climbing the slope bearing left into woodland. At the road turn right and almost immediately bear right again down a farm track. After two gates/stiles, leave the boundary and walk up a broad bank which gently bears round to the left, and above some trees. As the path turns into another valley, the chimneys of Cold Ashton can be glimpsed on the skyline.

Continue ahead over two more gates/stiles. Ahead again, but just before a bank on the right, look for a waymark post directing you to turn sharp (hairpin) right into a wooded gully. Follow this to a fence on the left, and turn left through a gate into a field. Follow the stream line on the right up the valley, veering left to a waymark post directing you diagonally right up the steep opposite bank. Over a stile, aim straight up the field to the buildings on the horizon. To the left can be seen the curved retaining wall for the forecourt of the Elizabethan Cold Ashton Manor.

The gate at the road marks the end of the Limestone Link and its junction with the Cotswold Way. Beckford's Tower on Lansdown above Bath is on the western skyline. Turn right along the road. (The Cotswold Way turns left into the churchyard and on to the White Hart on the A420.)

Beyond the cottages, ignore the first signpost on the right. Marshfield is seen on the horizon ahead. At the second signpost turn right into the field, bearing slightly left into the point of its lower hedge. Through a gate, descend the steep sided valley; turn left above a ruined hut. Beyond the gate, aim for a gap in the hedgeline ahead, then gently descend towards a stream and over a stile, and onto another.

The path moves to the other side of the streambed, and at a field corner bears right up the slope to a stile. Over this, turn left along a bridleway called Green Lane, turning left to Bellum farm buildings and beyond to the main street beside the tollhouse built to collect tolls on the turnpiked road.

Turn right to the village centre, passing the almshouses on the left, built in 1612 by Nicholas and Ellis Crispe of the Salters Company.

The almshouses built in Marshfield by the Crispe brothers.

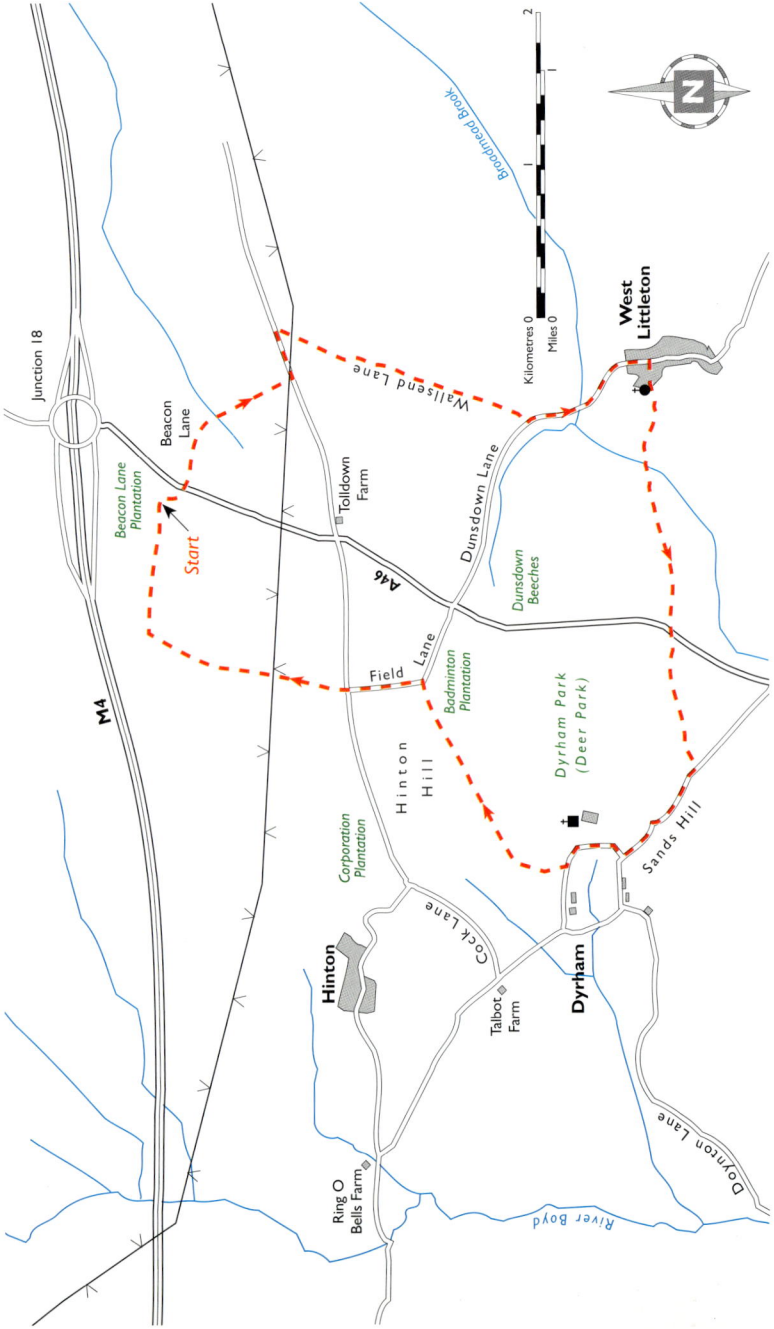

TORMARTON AND DYRHAM PARK

This walk combines the pleasures of a remoter Cotswold village with those of a grand estate.

Leave the Picnic Area by walking out the way you drove in, that is, by following the access road to the main road. Cross carefully to the signposted track on the opposite side. Ahead, take the right-hand gate/stile and enter an enclosed green lane (Beacon Lane), leading to a field. Walk beside the hedge on your right through two fields to the road.

Turn left, and then right, passing under a line of pylons along the signposted bridleway towards West Littleton. The path enters a walled track (Wallsend Lane) ending at a road. Turn left and follow this lane into West Littleton. Ahead, beyond the crossroads in the middle of the common, turn right at a signpost beside the wall. Walk into the churchyard. Pass the church with its conical tower, and cross a

The church at West Littleton.

stone stile. Beyond a horse jumping enclosure, walk through a wicket gate and bear right across the field to a white field gate.

Ahead, cross the ladder stile, and follow the wall-cum-hedge to a track. Turn left for a few yards and turn right into the field, but, instead of going straight across, bear half-left down to the bottom of the valley to a plank footbridge across a stream, fringed with wild flowers in summer. Then bear slightly right across the field to a stone stile at a bend in the field boundary above. Continue across the next field in the same direction, diverging from the left-hand hedge to reach a gap in the hedge to the right of a dip in the field. In

INFORMATION

Distance: 8 km (5 miles).

Start and finish: Tormarton Picnic Area on the west side of A46, south of M4 junction 18. National Trust members, and others paying admission charges, may wish to park at Dyrham Park (A46 entrance); leave the car park on its south side to join the walk partway round.

Terrain: Easy field walking, but prepare for mud. Boots or strong shoes recommended.

Time: Allow a good 3 hours.

Refreshments: Dyrham Park (admission charge). Note that access to the Park is from the main entrance on the A46.

Toilets: Tormarton Picnic Area (free). Dyrham Park (admission charge).

Opening hours: *Dyrham Park:* all year, 1200–1730 (dusk if earlier); *Dyrham House:* Apr-Oct daily, 1200–1730 except Thu and Fri. Admission charge (NT members free).

the next field, bear slightly left to reach the footpath signpost beside the A46.

Cross the A46 with care and enter the grounds of the Dyrham estate over the walled steps. Those parking at Dyrham will join the walk here.

(If you wish to visit the Park and House, instead of going over the wall, turn right, northwards, along the verge of the A46 to the main entrance, where you can pay the fee [National Trust members free], enjoy the Park and visit the House at the foot of the slope. To rejoin the walk, follow the car exit road near the House, and resume the description, turning right at the exit from the park.)

The path follows close to the wire deer fence on the right, outside the car park and parkland. Through the fence, deer are often seen (Dyrham is derived from deor-hamm, meaning 'deer enclosure'). At one point the roof of the east front of the House appears with the church tower behind.

At the field exit, the path bears diagonally left across a recent tree planting to a stile above the road. Turn right down this road (Sands Hill), which serves the village, and provides the return to the A46 for cars which have been visiting the House. Continue down the road, passing the exit from the Park.

As you enter the village, the Cotswold Way joins the road from the left. The route follows it back to the Picnic Area. At the triangular green, turn right following below the high wall of the garden of the House. Through the ornamental gates, the west façade is revealed.

William Blathwayt was Secretary of State at the end of the 17th century and start of the 18th. Contemporary diarist John Evelyn wrote 'This gentleman is Secretary of War, Clerk of the Council, etc., having raised himself by his industry from very moderate circumstances. He is a very proper, handsome person, very dextrous in business, and, beside all this, has married a great fortune . . .', which is what enabled him, at the turn of the 17th and 18th centuries, to build Dyrham House - or rather rebuild it, starting with the west front seen through these gates. This front by a French architect, Samuel Hauduroy, contrasts with the east front, built in more classical style by William Talman some years later. Talman was Sir Christopher Wren's principal assistant.

The east front looks up the scarp hillside beyond. Here, in the early 18th century, was a formal garden with a cascade, topped with a statue of Neptune. The garden fell into decay and by the early 19th century was laid out in the more open, sweeping 'Capability Brown' style typical of the period. All that remains of the original garden is Neptune.

The government bought the House in the 1950s and the Park in the 1970s, and transferred them to the National Trust. However, the Blathwayt family still have estates in Somerset, as drivers using the toll road to avoid Porlock Hill will know.

The walk passes the gates giving this view of Dyrham church and House.

Follow the road past the entrance to the church, which contains a memorial to George Wynter, ancestor of Mary Wynter, who married William Blathwayt, and turn right up the bridleway into the field above. Follow the park wall through four more fields. The Battle of Dyrham here in 577 was a turning-point, enabling the Saxons to drive the Britons westwards and occupy the Severn Vale to Gloucester.

Across the valley to the left are strip lynchets, a form of terracing allowing crops to be grown on steep land. The wall is heightened with deer fencing. Much of the stone was used to repair the more publicly seen walls elsewhere in the 1970s and 1980s.

At the road, turn left. Cross the next junction half-left onto the path beside the left-hand hedge through two fields (under the pylon line again). At the third field, turn right along the edge, by the woodland, rounding the corner to the left, and then right through the woodland to reach the Picnic Area.

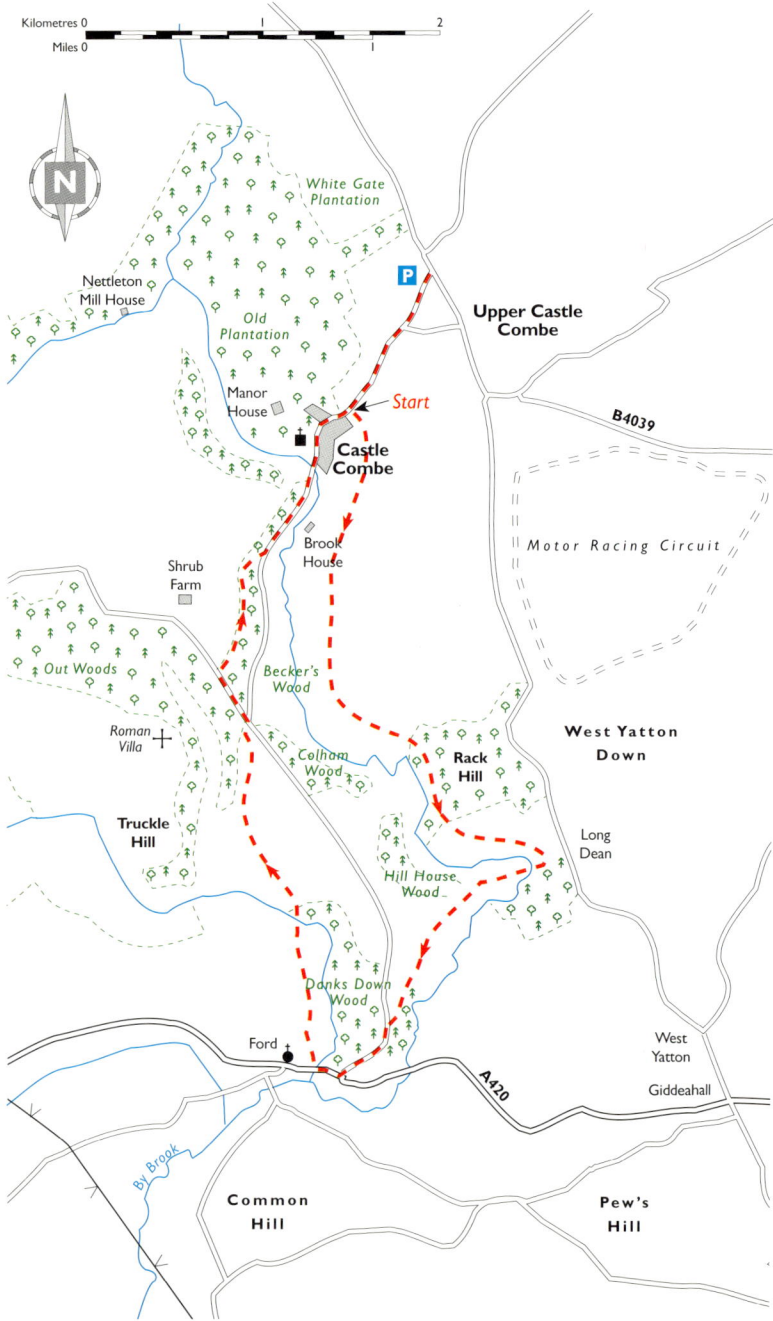

Kilometres 0   1   2

Miles 0   1

N

White Gate Plantation

Nettleton Mill House

Old Plantation

P

Manor House

Start

Castle Combe

Upper Castle Combe

B4039

Brook House

Motor Racing Circuit

Shrub Farm

Out Woods

Becker's Wood

Roman Villa

Colham Wood

Rack Hill

West Yatton Down

Truckle Hill

Hill House Wood

Long Dean

Danks Down Wood

Ford

A420

West Yatton

Giddeahall

By Brook

Common Hill

Pew's Hill

CASTLE COMBE

The village, in a steep wooded combe (valley), is reached at the end of the walk. The castle, to the north of the village, with its motte and baileys is long gone. Castle Combe merits the awards it has won for its beauty, which may be why it was chosen as a setting for the film of Dr Dolittle.

Much of the walk is through woodland and pasture, providing opportunities to enjoy the life cycles of different plant species. Ground plants like dog's mercury carpet the woodlands in early spring before the tree canopy shuts out the light. Beeches abound and in some years the seed, or mast, is prolific. Hedgerow shrubs such as hawthorn, blackthorn and elder provide brilliant white flowers in spring, changing to red haws, blue/black sloes and black elderberries in autumn. Pasture and scrub host limestone- loving flowers.

Between the upper and lower sections of road parking is a house which proclaims its birth date as 'Anno Domini MDCCCXXIII' or 1823. Opposite is a bridleway signposted to Upper Castle Combe. Follow this path up the track. Just beyond the point where another path joins from the right, turn right into woodland. Follow the path as it turns left on the edge of the wood, beside a field. Bearing right, and deeper into the woodland, pass between two stone pillars. The woodland becomes more mature and through the foliage to the right can be seen the roofs of the village and the church tower with its spire-like turret. Winter walkers, of course, get a better view.

There are more gateposts on the gentle descent and the path passes through an area of nature conservation interest for its limestone grassland and scrub. There are open areas where the extent of the combe can be seen. The path converges on another at the lower level and continues parallel downstream with the By Brook.

There is sturdy hazel coppice which would have provided many of the local needs, such as hurdles.

INFORMATION

Distance: 8 km (5 miles).

Start and finish: Public car park beside the B4039, north-west of Upper Castle Combe. This is reached from Chippenham westwards on A420 then B4039; from A46 Sodbury Cross Hands Hotel eastwards on B4040, then B4039. On less busy days it may be possible to park on lane down to Castle Combe. Park in upper, designated area.

Terrain: Gentle gradients apart from one short steep ascent in second half. No special footwear needed.

Time: Allow 3–4 hours.

Refreshments: Castle Combe: Castle and White Hart Inns; Ford: White Hart Inn, 200 m from route.

Toilets: Castle Combe: 75 m south of bridge, at end of walk.

Opening hours: *Castle Combe Museum:* Easter to 1 Oct, Sun and Bank Holidays, 1400–1700.

These shrubs can last a long time as they are cut to ground level periodically (coppiced) to stimulate new growth from the stump. Even collapsing dry stone walls provide homes for mosses, lichens, plants, insects and beetles.

Beyond the next stile, follow the track down into the settlement of Long Dean. Bear right on the lower track, passing to the right of Nut Tree Cottage. Cross the bridge over the By Brook as it meanders gently. The track passes more buildings through more woodland before emerging into a field. Follow the right-hand boundary until, after 200 m, it bears right. Here strike out left across the field towards its far corner enclosed by woodland.

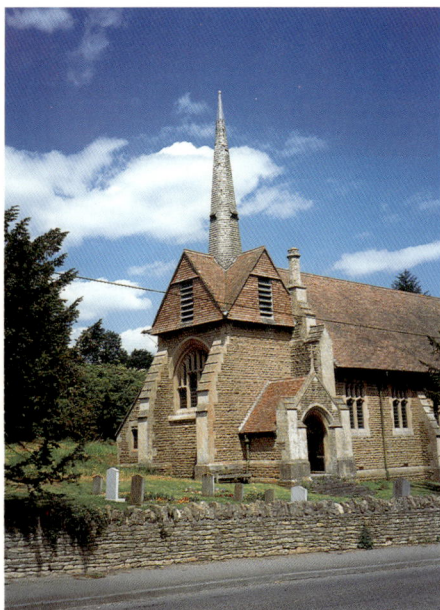

The church at Ford.

Turn left at the road, past another conservation area on the right, to reach the A420 and the village of Ford. Turn right and follow the footway, over a bridge, and turn right again into Park Lane.

A little further along the main road, the Colerne road bears left and takes you 200 m to the White Hart Inn, for refreshment if you wish. Return to Park Lane afterwards.

Pass Church Farm house on the right. At the top of the lane enter the field beyond and bear round to the right, then bearing left into woodland. The path emerges into a field. Follow the left-hand edge, and towards the end of the field, bear right down to the stream. This is a tributary of the By Brook, in a different combe. Cross the stream, bear left and, in the steep field beyond, ascend diagonally across the contours, into a strip of woodland, and the field above that. Stopping to admire the view, grassland flowers and the woodland helps recoup energy!

The path reaches the upper field boundary and follows it to the left. Above the woodland on the opposite hillside, half left ahead, lies the site of a Roman villa. Follow the path through the scrub of blackthorn or sloe, hawthorn and brambles. Autumn walkers might contemplate a feast of blackberry pies together with a bottle of gin flavoured with the sloes.

Cross the stile into woodland and continue to the road. Taking the path left, just inside the woodland, for 100 m avoids the road junction and brings you to a stile on the upper road (ignore the path disappearing further ahead). Turn left on the road (ignore the stile immediately opposite) and walk 50 m up to another stile on the right. Bear diagonally left in this mature beech woodland, later bearing right down the hill to meet the road.

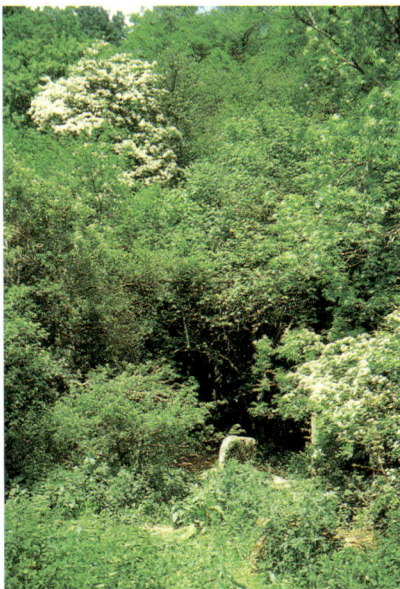

The curious elusive stile/bridge between Ford and Castle Combe.

Turn left on the road, over the bridge and walk into the village. Enjoy its church, market cross and the architecture as well as its facilities, before bearing right past the Castle Inn up the hill, passing the Museum, to your car.

Castle Combe.

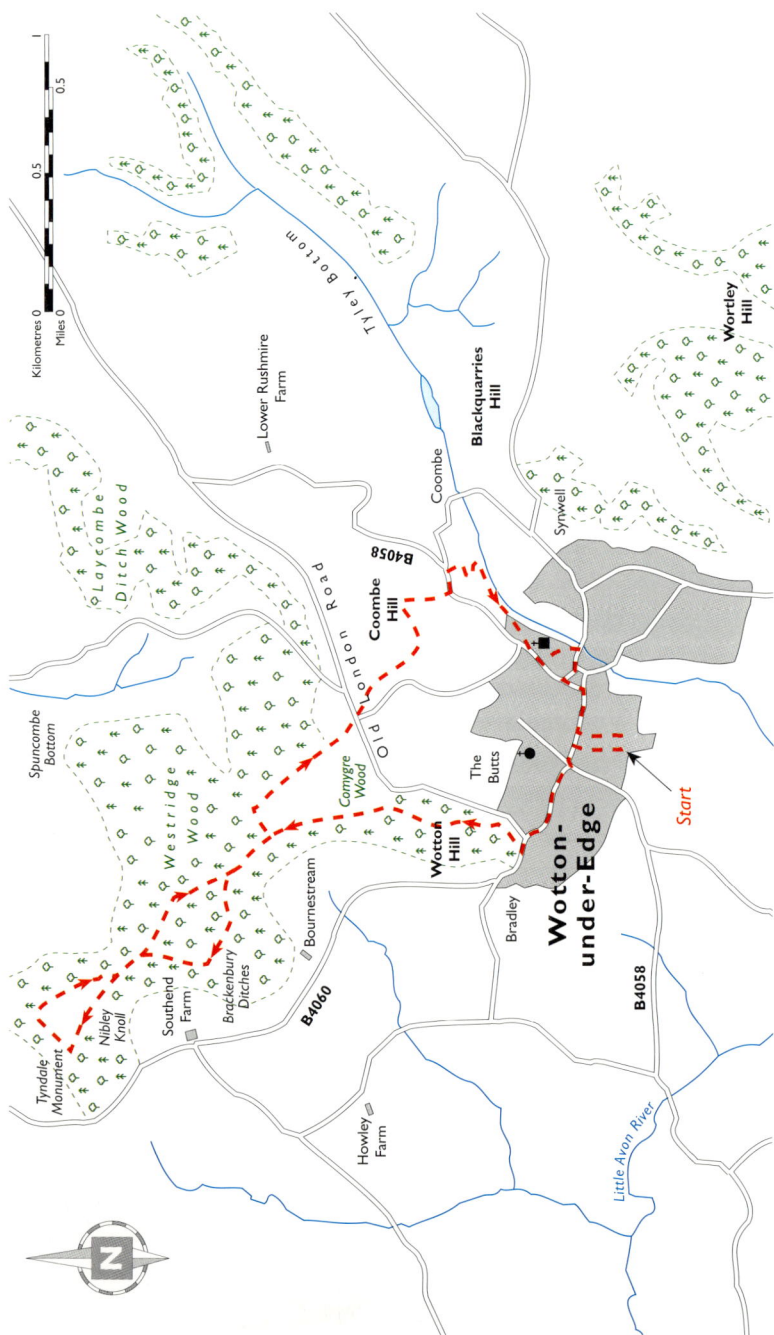

Kilometres 0
Miles 0

Tyley Bottom

Lower Rushmire
Farm

Laycombe Ditch Wood

Coombe

Blackquarries
Hill

Wortley
Hill

Synwell

B4058

Coombe
Hill

Old London Road

Spuncombe
Bottom

Westridge Wood

Cornygre Wood

The Butts

Wotton
Hill

Start

Wotton-
under-Edge

Bradley

Bournestream

Southend
Farm

Brackenbury
Ditches

Nibley
Knoll

Tyndale
Monument

B4060

Howley
Farm

B4058

Little Avon River

N

WOTTON UNDER EDGE

'**W**ood tun (homestead) under the (Cotswold) edge', now a lively town, contains many fine Cotswold features, like the church and nearby cottages. The Perry and Dawes Almshouses welcome you to a tranquil courtyard and chapel.

From The Chipping (a Scandinavian word meaning market), walk, appropriately, along Market Street. Turn left under the Jubilee Clock, honouring Queen Victoria's Diamond Jubilee in 1897. Cross the junction ahead into Bradley Street, and at its upper end bear right to the main road.

Turn left, pass Old London Road on the right, and cross over to a steep path with handrail, signed Cotswold Way. Climb up and, beyond a drive, cross a stile, turning left to a waymark post at the foot of Wotton Hill, with trees on top. Turn right and shortly bear left and climb up to them. The view opens out over the southern Severn Vale. The trees, originally planted to commemorate Wellington's victory at Waterloo in 1815, were replanted and walled in honour of Queen Victoria's Golden Jubilee in 1887.

Climbing again, leave the field at the top left-hand corner, crossing a stile into a cultivated field. Follow the left side, to join a bridleway coming from the right. Follow it ahead, now in the National Trust's Westridge Woods, with a hedge/tree line between you and the field on the right.

At the track junction, proceed half left on the Cotswold Way. The path bears right to stay on the level; avoid paths which descend the edge. Bear right at the next junction. On the left are the ditches and banks of the iron age fort of Brackenbury Ditches. The path bears generally right onto broad tracks, remaining close to the edge. As it turns, a view of the Tyndale Monument is seen through the trees to the left. The path bears left into woodland on its way to the Monument. After 300 m emerge into a field. Follow

INFORMATION

Distance: 8 km (5 miles).

Start and finish: The Chipping car park, off High Street, along Market Street. Wotton is on the B4058 Bristol-Nailsworth road and the B4060 Dursley-Chipping Sodbury road.

Public transport: Badgerline from Bristol, Stagecoach from Stroud.

Terrain: Scarp walking with a steep climb near the beginning and a steep descent towards the end. Boots recommended.

Time: Allow 3–4 hours.

Refreshment: Wotton under Edge: Inns and tearooms in the town.

Toilets: Wotton under Edge: Rope Walk, north-east corner of the Chipping car park, passed at the end of the walk.

the left-hand edge, to a topograph and the Monument itself. For a view from the top, the key can be obtained from North Nibley, the village 100 m (300 ft) below, but it has to be returned after viewing!

William Tyndale, born locally, was a tutor at Little Sodbury Manor before moving to London. He translated the Bible into English in the 1530s, thereby incurring the wrath of the Establishment. Eventually fleeing to Flanders, he was killed and burnt at the stake. Two years later, when Henry VIII had broken with Rome, an English translation was required. Miles Coverdale used much of Tyndale's work.

Primroses.

Leave the Cotswold Way to its steep stepped descent to North Nibley, and continue around the edge of the field to the right to a stile. Descend into woodland, bearing right then left along the quarry floor to a sunken track. Turn right. Go through the left-hand gate (bridleway – blue arrow), following the track round to the right past old quarries, with a view across them to the Monument. The track leads into the field, returning to the woodland.

Retrace your steps through the woodland for 300 m. At a waymark post, follow the blue arrow bearing left through the bushes to a track. Turn left for a few metres and bear right on another path, soon emerging into new plantations. Cross a track, and go over a stile into a second plantation. At the next stile, follow ahead into woodland to converge on the Cotswold Way (used on the outward journey). Bear left for 200 m.

At the junction turn left then right on a track following the field edge. Pass around a padlocked gate, and at the road, turn left. Just beyond the road on the right cross into a plantation (signed Coombe Hill). Bear right, following the track into open ground. Keep left and, beyond a gate, reach an electric pole at the top of a steep slope. Look beyond the trees below to see the strip lynchets, or terracing, on which the monks of Kingswood Abbey (near Wotton) grew their vines in medieval times.

Descend steeply, bearing slightly left to a clear path converging on the trees below. Join a track coming from the right. Continue ahead and follow the fence to cross a double stile. Walk down the strip lynchets, to a stile and the road below.

Cross the road, turn left, then right into a field (signed Holywell). At the bottom, turn right over a stile, and between houses to a road. Turn left for 100 m, and right on the Cotswold Way beside the stream. On reaching the road, continue ahead, then right to a main road. Turn left, and left again through the churchyard.

The present church was consecrated in 1283, on the site of earlier ones. Christ Church, Oxford, became its patrons at the Reformation; an example of Cotswold churches being controlled by big religious establishments elsewhere. It is a light and airy building, which has seen some alteration in its 700 years, including drastic, though not unpleasing, changes in the 19th century. The great local landowning family of the Berkeleys is commemorated by a brass representing Thomas who died in 1417, and his wife Margaret who predeceased him by 25 years.

Top: Wotton under Edge. Long Street with the Jubilee Clock celebrating 50 years of Queen Victoria's reign.

Bottom: Church Street, Wotton, with the Falcon Inn and the gabled front of the Almshouses beyond.

Leave the church through iron gates. Turn sharp left, then right at Shinbone Alley, leading to Church Walk and the main road.

Cross over into Church Street, passing the Perry and Dawes Almshouses on the left. Turn right up Long Street. Look for Rope Walk, an alley on the left (before reaching the Jubilee Clock), leading to the Baptist Church and The Chipping.

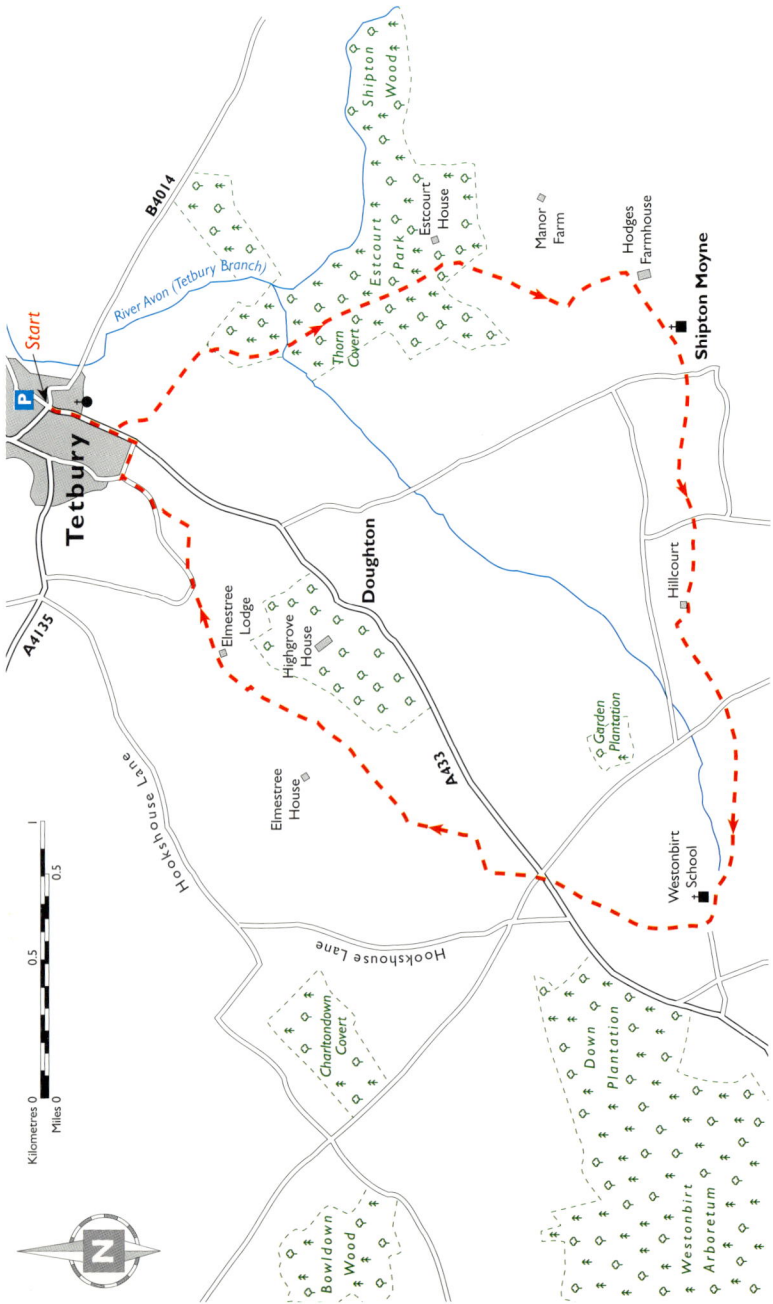

TETBURY

Antique-loving walkers may be long delayed in Tetbury! A busy Cotswold town, its market is still held beneath the arches of the Market House, which dates back to 1655. In the streets radiating from this point are many architectural treasures. Among them, the Snooty Fox (previously White Hart) was rebuilt in Jacobean style by Lewis Vulliamy in the 19th century, with an Assembly Room to accommodate the Beaufort Hunt. You see Vulliamy's work later, at Westonbirt.

The Chipping car park is on the site of an old market, as the name implies. At the other end of Market Place is the Talbot, once a tavern and now converted to dwellings, though its former use is given away by a moulded brewery plaque. North of the Talbot is Gumstool Hill, venue for the annual Woolsack Race held in May, when contestants have to carry heavy sacks up the 1 in 4 gradient, reflecting Tetbury's early prosperity from the wool trade.

Walk down Church Street. St Mary's Church was rebuilt in 1781, 'Victorianised' in 1901 and returned to its near-original Georgian form as recently as 1993. It has a surprisingly brilliant, light-filled interior with slender timber columns supporting the roof. An unusual feature is the passageway outside the nave, the only access to some of the pews.

INFORMATION

Distance: 13 km (8 miles).

Start and finish: Market House. Tetbury is reached from Bath on A46 and A433; from Cirencester on A433; from Stroud on A46 and A4135.

Car parking: The Chipping near the Market House, or Old Brewery Lane opposite St Mary's Parish Church.

Public transport: Alexcars from Cirencester.

Terrain: Easy, but longer walk, with little climbing, through parkland and farmland. Boots or strong shoes recommended.

Time: Allow 4–5 hours.

Refreshments: Tetbury: Inns and tearooms in the town. Shipton Moyne: The Cat and Custard Pot Inn.

Toilets: Tetbury: near both parking places.

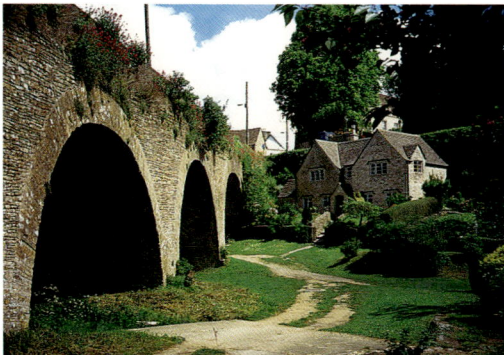

Tetbury's road bridge constructed 200 years ago to avoid the valley descent.

Turn right into West Street (the lower exit from the churchyard is opposite). After 50 m, go left down a path, passing under an arch supporting the road above. Turn right beside the arches, along the old road, superseded by the bridge two and a quarter centuries ago.

At the present road level, turn left over a stile. Follow the right-hand footpath. A rearward look reveals the ramparts of 'Tetta's bury' below the church. Beyond another stile, bear left beside the right-hand wall. Curiously the path is in the field, not in the lane to the right.

In the next field the path joins an avenue of recently planted trees. At double gates, cross the stone stile on the left, cross the track and go over a wooden stile, to follow the right-hand hedgeline. Cross another stile, and 100 m beyond, reach a gate. Turn right into a thicket of trees, then left and right over two bridges.

Tetbury Church towering above Tetta's bury.

Walk ahead across the parkland. Converge on the woodland on the right, and join the drive for Estcourt Park. Over a cattle-grid, walk straight past the buildings to another cattle-grid beside a lodge. Leaving the drive, turn right round the lodge to a gate in the hedge. Aim half left, for a stile midway in the wall ahead.

Beyond, cross to a stile in the wire fence. Half right again, cut the field corner to another stile. Turn left on the drive, turning right in front of the farmhouse, and through a gate. Aim for Shipton Moyne church ahead, and through the churchyard.

The church contrasts with the exhilarating flamboyance of Tetbury's in being a Victorian restoration along more usual Gothic lines. The Estcourt family chapel lists those heads of the family who have been interred here since the 14th century.

The "Cat and Custard Pot" at Shipton Moyne.

From the church, follow the drive to the main street. The path opposite passes to the left of the inn called the Cat and Custard Pot.

The odd name was bestowed by a director of the brewery which took over in the 1920s. He happened to be reading R. S. Surtees' 1840s book about the adventures of Mr Jorrocks, in which an inn of that name appeared. Cross three stiles, and bear half right to a small barn. Beyond, diverge from the left-hand boundary to a stone stile left of a gate. Follow the right-hand wall, first through a horse exercising area, then a field, to a road.

Across the road to the right, enter a field beyond the drive. Diverge from the left-hand fence through two gates, and bear right for the buildings of Hillcourt. Over a stile, pass through the farmyard, turning right onto the drive. Beyond the last building, turn left on a track past woodland and a house to a gate. Turn left but, instead of going through the next gate, turn right beside the fence. Beyond the next gate, pass close to the woodland on the right and reach the road.

Enter the field across the road, and aim for a gate set at an angle. Go through, bearing right to a stile. Beyond, diverge from the right-hand hedgeline, through a metal kissing gate. Bear slightly right across parkland, with a view of Westonbirt School, originally built by Lewis Vulliamy in the 1860s for the Holford family. He had already designed Dorchester House in Park Lane, London, for Holford – a building demolished to make way for the present Dorchester Hotel.

To the left of the school is the church. Aiming left of it, leave the field through a gate. Walk half right, cross two stiles and join the golf course. Bear half right across the course to the clubhouse. Follow the road beyond, below a garden with a variety of trees – a foretaste of the delights to be found in the famous Arboretum. Founded by R. S. Holford and now managed by the Forestry Commission, the Arboretum covers 240 hectares and includes many exotic trees. The spectacular displays vary from rhododendrons and azaleas in spring to the brilliant 'fall' colours of acers in October. The village in front of you was moved from near the church to enable the surroundings of the house to be enhanced with Italianate gardens.

Beyond a house, turn right into the parkland of Westonbirt School. Westonbirt Arboretum is over to the left. Cross a drive and bear left to a kissing gate. Pass to the right of a copse, through a gate, and on to the far corner. The Hare and Hounds Hotel is on the left.

Diagonally across the road junction, follow the signed path through trees, crossing the field to a gate/stile. Beyond, follow the left-hand hedgeline. After the gate on the left, turn left over a stile, heading diagonally up the slope to a stone stile 100 m left of the far corner. Again head diagonally to the far right-hand corner, entering an enclosed pathway to the right. Follow the right-hand hedge in the next field. Over a stone stile, head across two fields and cross the drive to Elmestree House, seen on the left.

To the left of a copse with a pool, go through gates, heading for another midway in the boundary. Beyond, aim for Elmestree Lodge. Continue along Longfurlong Lane past a farm. Turn right into a field and turn left, following the hedge. Over a track, enter the field ahead. Aim for the left side of a plantation. Crossing stile and footbridge, walk through the poplars to a stile on the left. Ascending the field parallel to the right-hand wall, reach the road beside a bungalow.

Turn right along the road, and right again to reach the A433 road. Turn left to cross the bridge back into Tetbury.

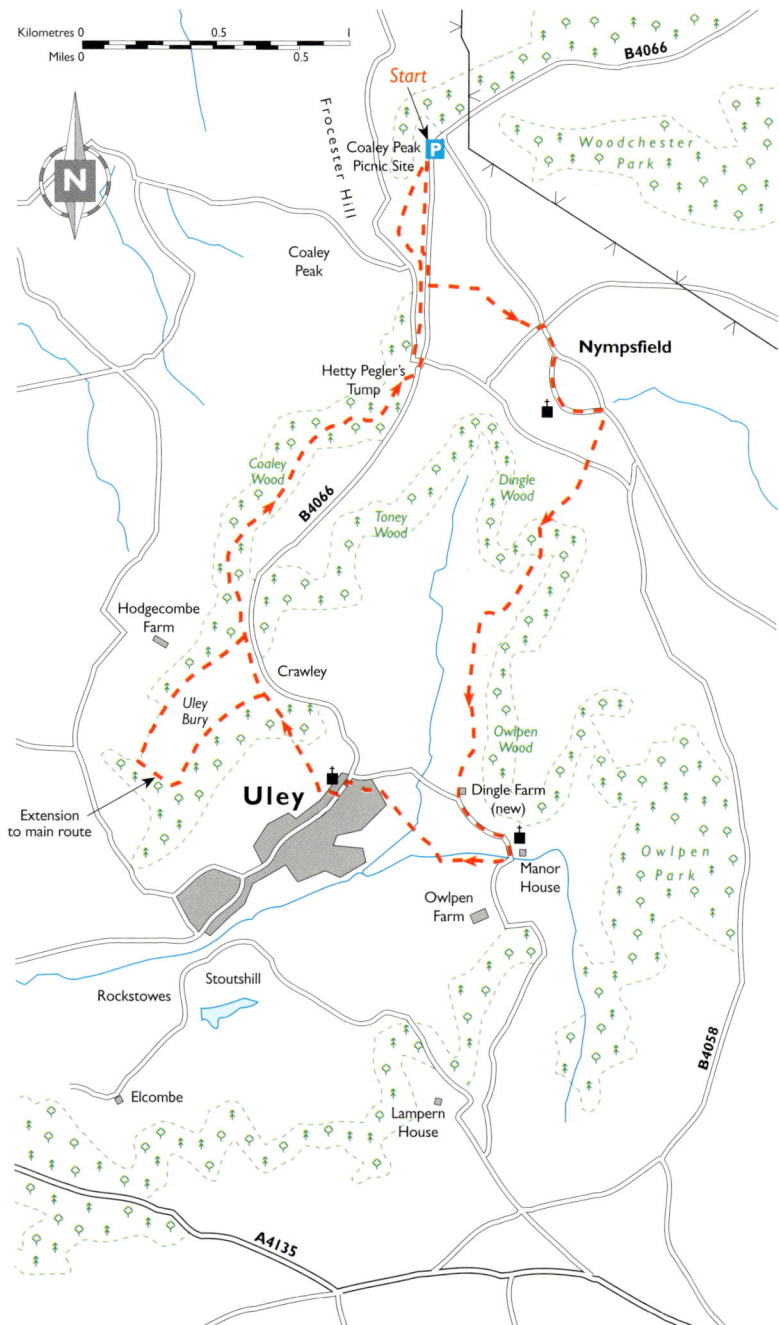

Kilometres 0   0.5   1
Miles 0   0.5

N

Start

Coaley Peak
Picnic Site

P

Coaley
Peak

Frocester Hill

B4066

Woodchester
Park

Nympsfield

Hetty Pegler's
Tump

Coaley
Wood

B4066

Toney
Wood

Dingle
Wood

Hodgecombe
Farm

Crawley

Uley
Bury

Owlpen
Wood

Dingle Farm
(new)

Extension
to main route

Uley

Owlpen
Park

Manor
House

Owlpen
Farm

Stoutshill

Rockstowes

Lampern
House

Elcombe

B4058

A4135

COALEY PEAK, OWLPEN AND ULEY

T he picnic site encourages you to dwell on the expansive view of the Vale of Severn, from the Severn Bridge in the south towards the estuary, up to Gloucester in the north, with the enormous bends in the river in front and the Forest of Dean behind. On the site itself is an example of a prehistoric long barrow, and the walk explores high plateau and hidden valleys behind the scarp. It includes the three churches of the United Benefice of Uley cum Owlpen and Nympsfield – all largely Victorian replacements for earlier dilapidated places of worship.

Walk along the upper edge of the field (beside the road), southwards to the corner and, beyond the young beech trees, a kissing gate. Bear left to the road. Turn right for 50 m; cross and follow the signposted footpath on the left. Follow the boundaries, first on the right, then left, through two fields to a road. Turn left, and right at the cross roads into Nympsfield.

Pass the Rose and Crown on the right and follow the right-hand, upper, lane to St Bartholomew's church. The original foundation dates back to about 1090. It was controlled by Gloucester Abbey until the Reformation, when it became a Crown living. Pictures inside show the dilapidated church immediately prior to the rebuilding in the 1860s.

Samuel Teulon's design is a Victorian, but pleasing representation of the medieval, and blends with the late 15th century tower, which was retained. The difficulties of making a living here seem to be reflected in an ancient rhyme quoted in the church:

'Nympsfield is a pretty place
built upon a tump,
But what the people live
upon is heg peg dump.'

INFORMATION

Distance: 9 km (6 miles).

Start and finish: Coaley Peak Picnic Site on B4066, south of Stroud (on Cheltenham-Wotton under Edge Scenic Route). Park to left of entrance.

Terrain: Undulating field and woodland walking, with two moderately strenuous ascents in second half. Boots or strong shoes recommended.

Time: Allow 3–4 hours.

Refreshments: Nympsfield: Rose and Crown; Uley: Old Crown.

Toilets: At start; north end of picnic site.

Opening hours: *Owlpen Manor:* 1 Apr-30 Sept, Tue, Thu, Sun and Bank Holidays, plus Wed in July and Aug, 1400–1700. Admission charge.

Nympsfield bus shelter in Cotswold style

'Heg peg dump' is thought to be berries from the hedgerow.

Follow the lane past the church, and turn right at the junction. After 100 m, turn right on the footpath which climbs the field. Continue to a stone stile, and ahead on a short track to a road. Cross this and go over the stile opposite. The path descends, converging on the bottom right-hand corner. Cross the stile, and turn left to a stile/gate into woodland. Take the centre path, bearing right, down the ravine. Cross a stile into a field and follow the valley bottom, between Owlpen Wood (left) and Dingle Wood (right). The path bends right, revealing Uley on the far right-hand hillside.

Keep to the upper path beside the left-hand hedge. Below right, the pond is one of the spring sources feeding the River Ewelme, which rises in the combe beyond. Dingle Farm, shown here on old maps, has vanished. Continue into the field with the hedge on the right, reaching the road, by the new Dingle Farm.

The church and the manor house at Owlpen.

Turn left. Pass the Owlpen Manor entrance and take the next turn left to the church. This again is a Victorian reconstruction, started in the 1830s with a number of changes and additions over the next 40 years. The most notable feature is the extensive mosaic work in the chancel. On a gloomy day, press the timed light switches to see it clearly.

From the porch, follow the wall to the right, then left down to the Court House and the road. Turn left, and left again, near the letter box, onto a signed footpath for 50 m to view the south front of the Manor. Of medieval origin, Owlpen Manor is regarded as an outstanding Tudor house. It sits comfortably and satisfyingly below the church, with woodland as a backdrop to both. In the mid 19th century it fell into decay, but in 1926, Norman Jewson, who belonged to the group of craftsmen based on Sapperton, bought it and restored it.

Returning to the road, continue ahead to a gateway on the right. Follow the path through the gate and parallel to the right-hand hedge to a stile. Continue beyond to another. Over this, immediately turn right to cross a clapper bridge across the stream.

Walk straight across to a stile and stepping stones across a brook. Ascend, converging on a large tree and a hedge from the left (the tree-covered summit of Crawley Hill is above). Beyond the stile, the enclosed path leads onto the green at 'The Pink House' in Uley.

Turn left, pass the Old Crown, and cross the road into the churchyard with another 'modern' church – only a century and a half old. Leave the churchyard through the wall above it, turning left beside it. Ignoring the first turn right, take the second, a narrow enclosed path beside a bungalow.

Climb up towards the left flank of the woodland. Through the gate the path rises to the edge of Uleybury iron age hillfort. Turn right along the track below the hillfort ramparts, and ahead down to the road. (If you wish to extend the walk by 2 km, turn left instead, following the track round the other three sides of the hillfort, rejoining by turning left on the track to the road.)

Turn left through the gates, and immediately right onto a bridleway. Within a few paces, bear right on the upper path, signed Cotswold Way, which you follow for the rest of the walk.

Eventually descending a flight of steps, cross muddy tracks before bearing right above Knapp Cottages, and into an open tarmac area. Turn right and climb up Knapp Lane to the B4066 road. Turn left along the slip road (take care – cars drive fast here to reach Frocester Hill).

Turn left down the hill for 100 m, and turn right onto a path through old quarries. At the open ground, follow the scarp edge to the topograph, which indicates many features in the vale landscape and further away into Wales.

Walk from the topograph to the kissing gate in the fence above and return to the Picnic Site.

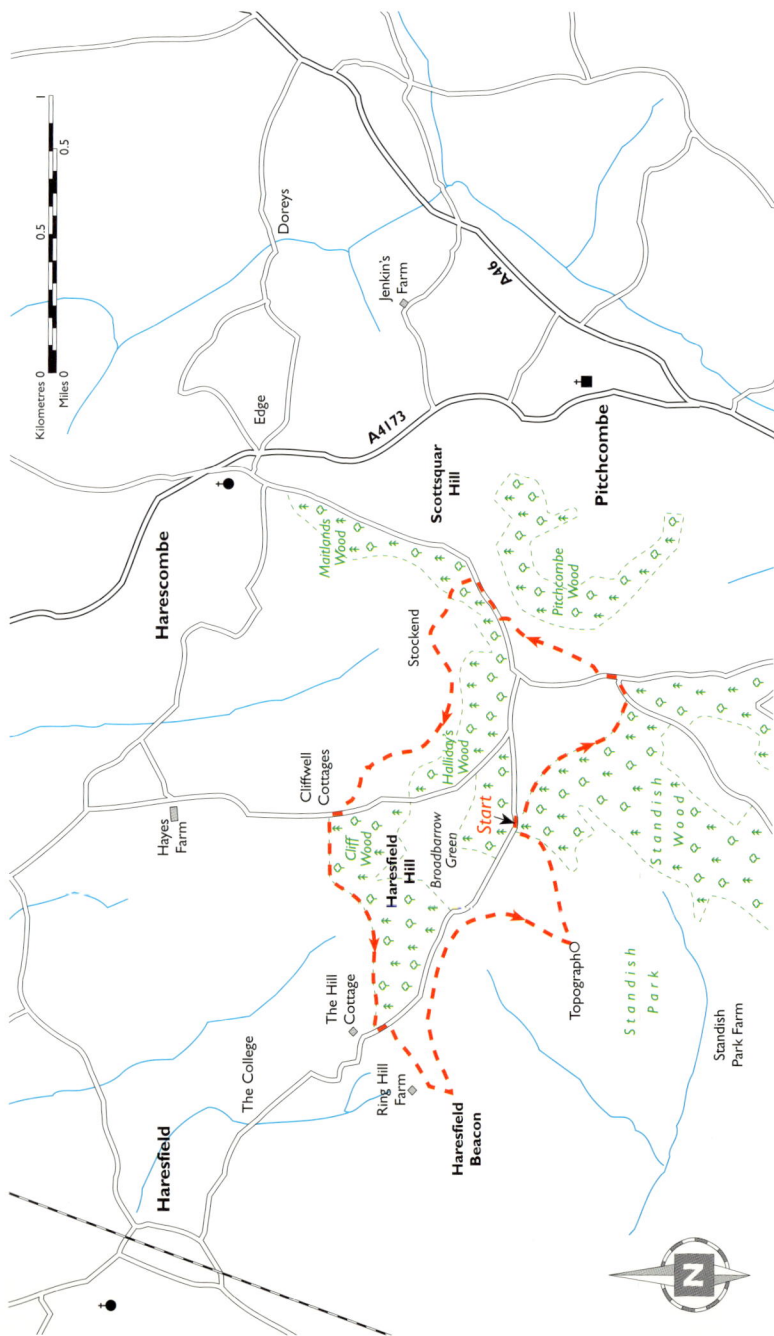

Kilometres 0
Miles 0

0.5

0.5

0.5

Doreys

Edge

Jenkin's
Farm

A46

A4173

Scottsquar
Hill

Pitchcombe

Harescombe

Maitlands
Wood

Pitchcombe
Wood

Stockend

Cliffwell
Cottages

Halliday's
Wood

Standish
Wood

Hayes
Farm

Cliff
Wood

**Haresfield
Hill**

Broadbarrow
Green

Start

Topograph

The Hill
Cottage

The College

Haresfield

Ring Hill
Farm

**Haresfield
Beacon**

Standish
Park

Standish
Park Farm

N

HARESFIELD BEACON

From the car park you can glimpse some of the view down the Severn Vale - reserved for the end of the walk!

Just outside the entrance to the car park is a walking-man signpost pointing into the woodland. Follow it with the wall on your right (do not follow the Cotswold Way on the other side of the wall, and ignore stiles giving access to it further on). After the woodland, walk along the edge of the field, to a road.

Turn left and, beyond the junction, cross to a footpath signpost at a stone squeeze stile, and walk straight across to another to the right of the right-hand radio transmitter in the woodland ahead.

Turn right, then left into the woodland. The path bears to the right, descending steeply in places and eventually converges on a track below. Turn right for 100 m (Cotswold Way). Just before the buildings, turn left down a grassy path, bearing left through another strip of woodland and then down a small field beside a fence. A high gate and fenced path lead to a road.

Turn left on the drive towards Randall's Farm, but before the ways part for the farm buildings and the house, bear left beside the trees, and into the field. The

INFORMATION

Distance: 7 km (4 miles).

Start and finish: Cripplegate car park (National Trust) on Edge-Haresfield road. From Stroud, take minor road north through Whiteshill. From Gloucester, take A4173, bearing right at Edge church onto minor road.

Terrain: Woodland and farmland. Some short moderately steep descents and ascents. Muddy in places. Boots or strong shoes recommended.

Time: Allow 2–3 hours.

Refreshments: None en route. Pubs in nearby villages.

Standish woods.

path curves gently to the right, over three stiles. The views here are northwards towards Gloucester and its cathedral and the Malverns beyond. At the fourth field, walk across towards the right-hand corner and through a gate, and bear left above the buildings of Tump Farm. Over a stile and into the farm drive, bear left up to the curiously named Pound of Candles Lane.

Across the lane to the right are Cliffwell Cottages. In front of them the Cotswold Way (which you follow to the end of the walk) leads off to the left. At the start is an old well – Cliff Well – in its own 'house', with a thoughtful inscription on the wall:

DEO GRATIAS

Who'er the bucket full upwindeth,
Let him bless God who water findeth.
Yet water here but small availeth,
Go seek that well which never faileth.

. . . which is just as well, as the well-head is sealed with concrete!

The path passes the Siege Stone, commemorating the 1643 Royalist siege of Parliamentarian Gloucester in

View over the River Severn from Haresfield Beacon.

the Civil War. At the road at Ring Hill Farm, turn left and shortly right above the farm to climb the flank of Ring Hill, an iron age hill fort. Passing to the right of a field gate, the path reaches a stile and the open land of Haresfield Beacon. The familiar shaped Ordnance Survey trig pillar appears ahead; this one is made of Cotswold stone instead of the usual concrete.

The view to the right is obscured by trees, so move forward a little to enjoy the panorama over the widening Vale of Severn. The Cotswold scarp to the left resembles a coastline with promontories projecting like sea cliffs, the furthest visible being Stinchcombe Hill. The Forest of Dean is on the right across the river.

In between, the blocks of the Berkeley and Oldbury nuclear power stations are by the river. Beyond rise the piers of the old and new Severn Bridges. The radio tower at Ozleworth is on the skyline, half-left, with a similar tower in the Forest of Dean on the right. You will also notice the smaller radio tower to the left in Standish Wood nor far from the car park.

Run your eye along the skyline to the left of Stinchcombe Hill to see the tower of the Tyndale Monument above North Nibley, honouring the translator of the Bible into English (Walk 5).

Below the skyline is a long flat-topped hill called Cam Long Down. Local legend, similar to others elsewhere, has it that the Devil, incensed by the God-fearing people of Gloucestershire and their fine churches, resolved to dam the Severn and drown them. Filling his barrow with rock he set off but soon tired and enquired of a passing cobbler how far away the Severn was. The cobbler, with all the boots and shoes collected for repair strung round his neck, sensed something sinister and said he had worn them all out walking from the river. The Devil gave up, emptied out his barrow and formed Cam Long Down! It is also locally called Dough Trough, from a likeness to a loaf of bread.

Snowdrops.

Double back along the other flank of the hill to reach a road. Immediately turn right down steps and left along the contour beside a wall. The path rises through woodland and out into the open again. Bear right to reach the topograph set up in the 1930s, shortly after acquisition by the National Trust.

Double back along the other side of the promontory to the car park.

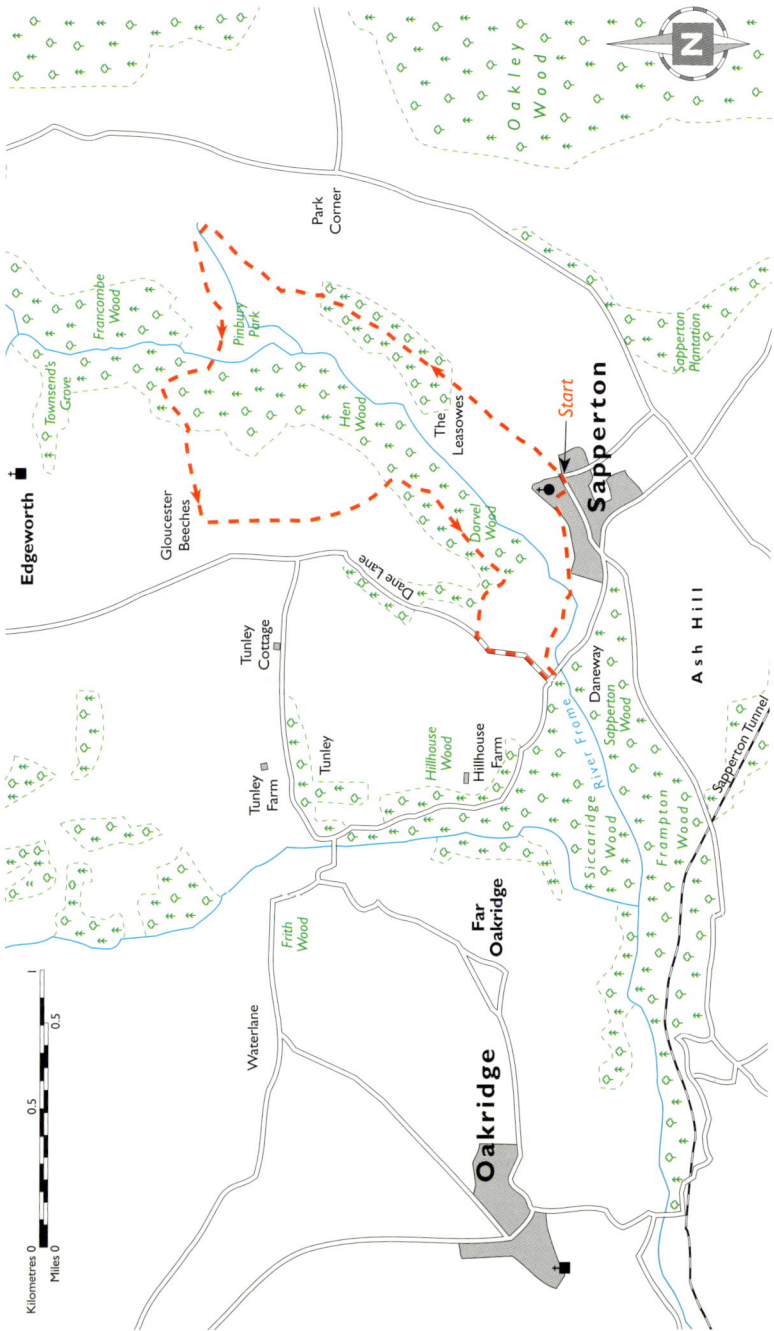

Oakley Wood

Sapperton Plantation

Park Corner

Francombe Wood

Pinbury Park

Townsend's Grove

Hen Wood

The Leasowes

Start

Sapperton

Edgeworth

Gloucester Beeches

Dorvel Wood

Dane Lane

Ash Hill

Tunley Cottage

Daneway

Sapperton Wood

Sapperton Tunnel

Tunley

Hillhouse Wood

Hillhouse Farm

River Frome

Siccaridge Wood

Frampton Wood

Tunley Farm

Far Oakridge

Frith Wood

Waterlane

Oakridge

Kilometres 0
Miles 0

0.5

0.5

SAPPERTON

S apperton, 'soap makers tun or homestead', is at the western end of the Broad Ride from Cirencester Park (Walk 10). A hundred years ago the Barnsley brothers, Sidney and Ernest, and Ernest Gimson came to Sapperton to develop their

Sapperton church.

Pinbury Park.

architectural and furniture making skills. They leased Pinbury Park from Lord Bathurst until his family needed it, when he provided land in Sapperton for them to build upon. A hundred years earlier still, the tunnel running below the western end of the village was built as part of the Thames-Severn Canal, which, with the Stroudwater Canal, linked the two great commercial waterways.

From the telephone box near the church, follow the signed bridleway through five fields, keeping fairly close to the wall on the right. With a house below left, continue ahead into the woodland, emerging beyond into a long pasture field.

The woodland on the left, called The Leasowes, is on the banks of the River Frome which rises, as do several

Cotswold rivers, just behind the western scarp. Running southwards to Sapperton, it then turns westwards into the steep-sided Golden Valley to Stroud and out to the River Severn, at Framilode near Frampton on Severn.

At the end of the field, descend to a gate, and bear round to the right parallel with the trees. Pinbury Park is seen across the valley. Bear left between the telegraph poles to reach a double gate, beyond which turn left, passing a small lake, and up to the drive to the house. Turn left on the drive and follow it past the house to reach a track beyond.

Descend the track bearing to the left, keeping to the right at the next junction. The path crosses the stream bed and enters a field. From the first gate, follow the left-hand hedge for 100 m to a second gate and enter the woodland. The path rises and turns to the left, eventually emerging at a gate beside the remains of Pinbury Cottages into an open field. Follow the right-hand wall line to a gate. Go through and turn left immediately to follow the left-hand wall down this field and the next to another bridleway junction.

The valley view from Pinbury Park.

Walk half-left across the field towards a gate into the woodland. The woodland path bears right, down towards the valley bottom but, before reaching it, turn right on a cross path through the more open woodland of Dorvel Wood, which allows more light to penetrate the canopy, benefitting lower growing plants such as spindle and wayfaring trees, bramble and fireweed. Ash saplings will also thrive. At another junction the path turns right and eventually emerges at a track, bounded on the left by recently rebuilt drystone walls.

Where the track reaches the road (Dane Lane) turn left along it, passing the grounds of Daneway House on the left. 'Dane' may promt visions of invaders from Europe, but comes in fact from Old English 'denu' meaning a valley. So you are in fact on the Daneway, the 'way up the valley'. Daneway House, of medieval origin, was lent to the Barnsleys and Gimson at the beginning of the 20th century for workshops and showrooms for their craft work.

Turn left again at the junction at the Daneway Inn. Over the bridge, turn immediately left on the path which follows the right-hand bank of the Thames-Severn Canal. The inn car park is built on a filled-in portion of the canal. The path, gravelled here, passes over a stile, entering a nature reserve of the Gloucestershire Wildlife Trust, and continues between the canal on the left and the River Frome on the right.

The canal bears right and passes a derelict cottage. The portal to the tunnel is ahead. Take the upper path in order to walk across the top of the portal. The stonework here used to be castellated parapet. It may in future be repaired by the Cotswolds Canal Trust, which has taken over the work of restoring the canal. The other portal, two miles away near Coates, has been restored, as has a section of the canal itself.

The canal was constructed in the late 18th century and was inspected by King George III in 1788. Flourishing for a while, it eventually declined in competition with the new and faster railways. A railway tunnel parallels the canal tunnel to the west. Gloucestershire County Council attempted to revive its fortunes in the early 1900s but it was not commercially viable and was eventually abandoned.

The Canal Trust is restoring sections, but it will be a long time before the whole length can be reopened. Much has disappeared and been incorporated into adjacent farmland in the eastern section. After so many years leaving nature to take over, there may be disagreement about restoring the canal to recreational activity when so much valuable wildlife habitat has been created.

From the stile above the portal, bear half right up the field to a stile below the woodland. Bear left, keeping the wire fence on the left, until the path emerges between walls and onto a lane. Turn left and then right beside the churchyard, a mass of snowdrops in the spring, to return to the start.

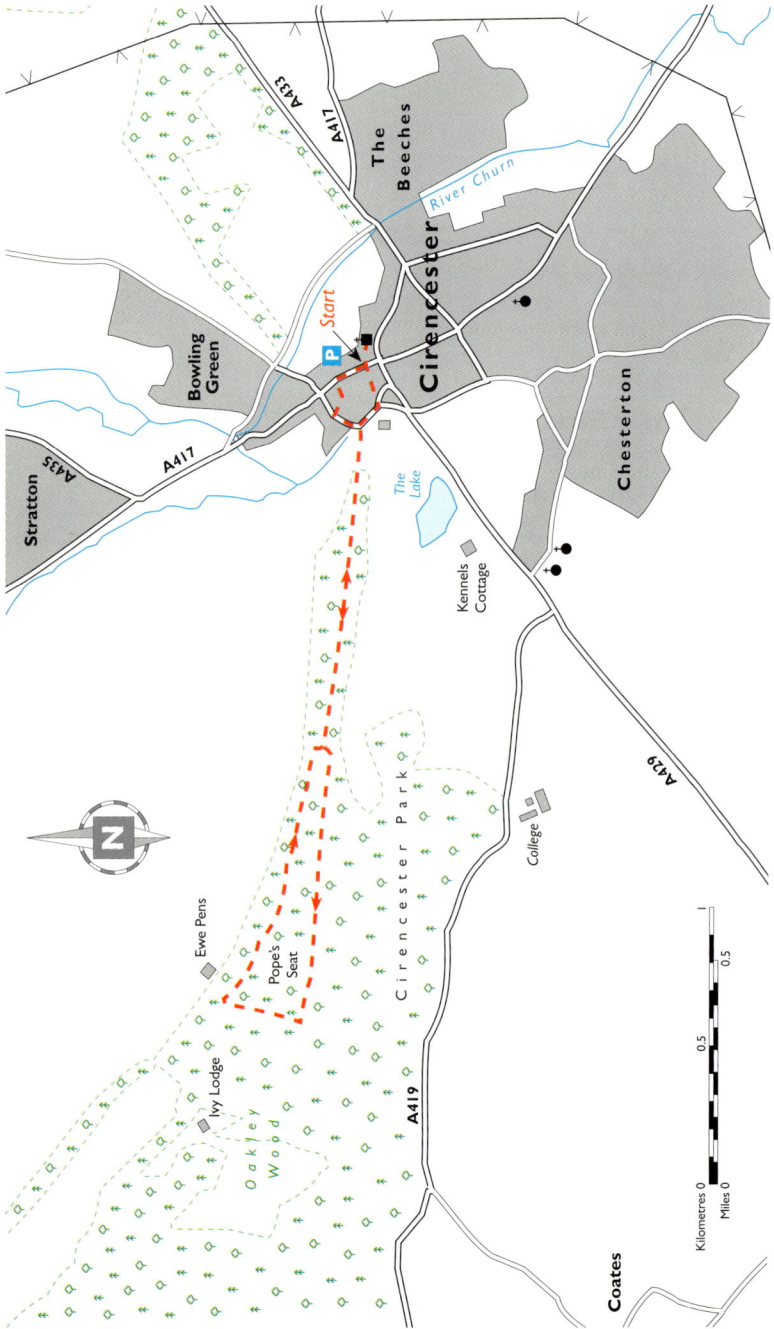

Start

P

The Beeches

A433

A417

River Churn

Cirencester

Bowling Green

Chesterton

Stratton

A435

A417

The Lake

Kennels Cottage

A429

Cirencester Park

College

Ewe Pens

Pope's Seat

Ivy Lodge

Oakley Wood

A419

Coates

N

Kilometres 0   0.5   1
Miles 0   0.5

CIRENCESTER PARK

irencester (Corinium) was the second largest city in Roman Britain. The Fosseway (Lincoln to Devon) and the Ermin Way (Gloucester to Silchester) cross here, and Akeman Street connects eastwards with Bicester, another Roman station. The Romans built roads as straight as they could. This walk is mostly straight too, on the Broad Ride of Cirencester Park. The House is not open.

Cirencester from the Park.

Start at the parish church in the market place. Previous churches may have been a little way away on a site occupied by the Abbey, founded about the same time. However, the Abbey has now disappeared, though you can walk over its site in the Abbey Grounds just north of the present church, which was founded in the early 12th century by Henry I.

There have been many alterations and additions since. The Early English nave was replaced in Tudor style in the early 16th century. The tower was built on the proceeds of loyalty to Henry IV around 1400 (the townspeople beheaded two rebel earls and were rewarded with their treasure). The porch was built at the turn of the 15th and 16th centuries, probably to provide offices over it as well as an entrance, and has been restored a number of times since.

There are many monuments in the church and a number of brasses commemorating notable people

INFORMATION

Distance: 6 km (4 miles).

Start and finish: Cirencester parish church porch, in the market place. Cirencester is at the crossing of the Fosseway (A429) and Ermin Way (A417).

Car parking: Long stay car parks are signposted.

Public transport: Stagecoach services from Cheltenham, Swindon and Stroud.

Terrain: Easy parkland walking, with a woodland ride. No special footwear needed.

Time: Allow 2–3 hours.

Refreshments: Wide choice in Cirencester.

Toilets: Several places in Cirencester.

Opening hours:
Corinium Museum: Daily, all year, except winter Mondays. Apr-Oct Mon-Sat 1000–1700, Sun 1400-1700, Nov-Mar Tue-Sat 1000–1700, Sun 1400–1700. Cirencester Park's opening hours are shown at the gates. Closing time could be as early as 1700, even in the summer. Make sure you have sufficient time for the whole walk.

Note: Dogs are welcome in Cirencester Park, and off the lead too when away from the lodge houses, but they are not allowed beyond the first part of the Broad Ride.

during the great medieval age of the wool trade. The children's guide suggests you look in the Lady Chapel for the forerunners of Tom and Jerry!

From the porch, walk round the end of the church beneath the tower. Continue ahead up Gosditch Street with the Abbey Grounds wall on the right. Turn left into the narrow Coxwell Street, and step back 300 years, into the world of great religious and political upheaval which culminated in the Civil War. Much of the architecture is 17th century, with some later 'facelifts' and a modern intrusion.

Turn left into Thomas Street and right up Cecily Hill, gradually coming more up to date, reaching the 1850s armoury called the Barracks with its tower. Passing through the Park gates, note the closing time and any requests.

The Park is idyllic and the public have been admitted for nearly 300 years, since the Bathurst family laid it out in the early 18th century. The walk as described may be thought by the more adventurous as too easy – a 'granny walk'. However, most of the rest of the Park is open to explore, subject to any requirements at the time, such as polo, country fairs and other events. The woodlands flanking the Broad Ride are extensive (5 sq km) so getting lost is easy. Mapreaders can navigate with the OS Pathfinder maps for Stroud and Cirencester (Nos 1113 and 1114), which show the rides.

It is a working estate. It has its own sawmill which uses the timber for fencing, gates and garden furniture.

Walk ahead straight up the Broad Ride, a grand avenue of mature trees, many of them horse chestnuts. The stone pavilion, the 'Hexagon', on the right provides a shelter in wet weather.

The avenue rises to the horizon, only to reveal more ahead. The Ride stretches another 6 km to the village of Sapperton, and a further kilometre beyond, outside the Park, to the valley of the River Frome.

Pope's Seat in Cirencester Park.

The grassy ride, still an avenue, becomes more informal. Pope's Seat on the right – another useful shelter – commemorates the involvement of the poet Alexander Pope in the design of the Park. At this meeting place of Seven Rides the area opens out. On the right is a square tower and the Park's polo ground. At the road which crosses the ride, the route reaches its furthest point before return.

(If you wish to complete the Broad Ride, bear in mind that it is nearly another 5 km there and the same back. Add on another 2–3 hours and remember the Park's closing time.)

Turn right on the road to the Round Tower, a romantic cottage, and enter the woodland, bearing right at a cross-roads. The mature beech trees tower above like cathedral columns, just some of those in the Park said to be amongst the finest in England.

The road bears right and into the Broad Ride. Turn left and retrace your steps back towards the town. The church tower rises beyond the Park. There may be a display of the estate sawmill's products near the gates.

Walk down Cecily Hill and turn right into Park Street, with the high estate walls on the right. At the left turn into Black Jack Street is the Corinium Museum, where you can learn more from the displays about Roman times and about the later history of the Cotswolds and the wool trade.

As you walk along Black Jack Street, look back to see the massive hedge in front of Cirencester Park, before reaching Gosditch Street near the start of the walk.

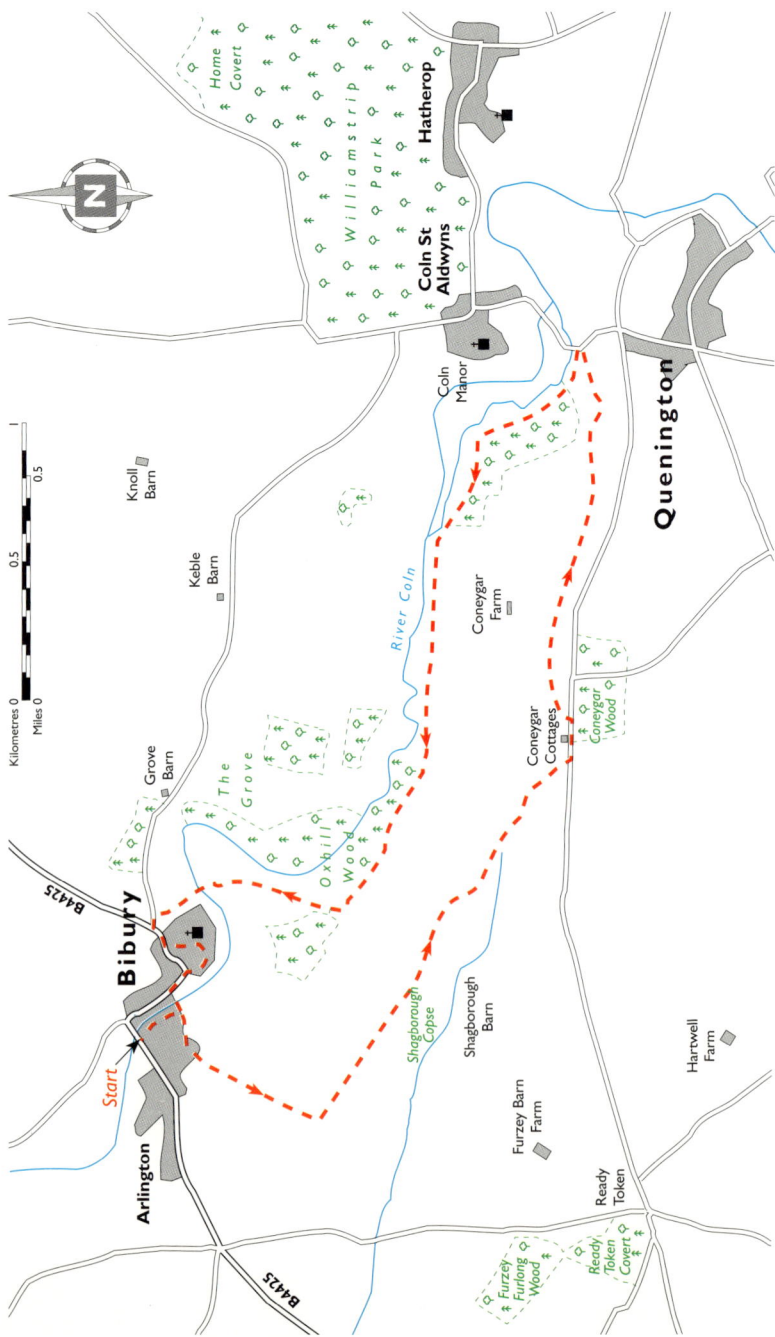

Kilometres 0

Miles 0

Home Covert

Williamstrip Park

Hatherop

Coln St Aldwyns

Coln Manor

Quenington

Knoll Barn

Keble Barn

River Coln

Coneygar Farm

Coneygar Cottages

Coneygar Wood

Grove Barn

The Grove

Oxhill Wood

Shagborough Copse

Shagborough Barn

Furzey Barn Farm

Hartwell Farm

Ready Token

Ready Token Covert

Furzey Furlong Wood

B4425

Bibury

Start

Arlington

B4425

BIBURY

Bibury is a classic Cotswold village, with its centre around the church, reached towards the end of the walk. The parish includes Arlington on the other side of the river.

From Arlington Mill take the path opposite, beside the stream which used to be the mill race, and which now cuts off Rack Isle, originally used for drying cloth on racks or tenters. The cloth was stretched on hooks, hence the expression 'being on tenterhooks'. Now a nature reserve owned by the National Trust, it is managed by the Gloucestershire Wildlife Trust.

Ahead, Arlington Row started life as a medieval store, later being converted into cottages for weavers, and now lived in by tenants of the National Trust. Turn right up the slope, known as Awkward Hill. At the top bear left to pass between houses and out to a field gate. Continue ahead to another gate. Arlington is seen to the right. Continue ahead with the field boundary on your right.

At the next junction of tracks, a helpful homemade signboard indicates ahead for 'Token' (meaning Ready Token – once a pub), and right for 'Pike' (Arlington Pike – turnpike house on the Cirencester to Burford road). You turn left, towards Coln St Aldwyns.

INFORMATION

Distance: 8 km (5 miles).

Start and finish: Arlington Mill. Bibury is on the B4425 Cirencester-Burford road.

Car parking: Beside river, east of Swan Hotel.

Terrain: Easy riverside and field edge walking, but Cotswold clay can be muddy! Boots or strong shoes recommended.

Time: 2–3 hours.

Refreshments: Tearooms in Bibury.

Opening hours: *Arlington Mill:* Easter to Christmas Eve, daily 1000–1800, admission charge.

The classic Cotswold cottages at Arlington Row

This track is probably an old road. The hedge is on the right for two fields, and left for the next two. Few dwellings are to be seen and the feeling is of the high open wold, which would have been sheep walks before enclosure two centuries ago. The enclosures prompted the building of isolated farmsteads to manage the new fields.

In the valley to the right is Shagborough Copse; the path converges on the end of it. Pass through the gates and out into a pasture field at the bottom of the slope. As the path climbs again, look back to see a valley without a stream. The porous rock below allows water to run below ground. Some such streams break to the surface after heavy rainfall. Near this point, the Roman Akeman Street passed on its way from Bicester to Cirencester, two important Roman military bases.

The path at Shagborough Copse.

Through another gate, continue to the road. Turn left and beyond the pair of houses (Coneygar Cottages) bear left on a bridleway. Do not hug the woodland edge, but strike out across the field to the left-hand side of the barns ahead right. Nearer the barns, a metal field gate at an angle takes the path between the barns and a house. Further to the left is seen Coneygar Farm, with an arc of trees to break the winds from north-west to north-east.

Through a gateway and across the middle of two fields, the path reaches the corner of a walled enclosure. Through the gate, follow the wall on your right. The walling stones in this eastern part of the Cotswolds are often much thinner than elsewhere. The path lies ahead in the woodland; through another gateway, turn left downhill to the river. Coln St Aldwyn village is on the hillside ahead and to the right.

Turn left at the junction for the return footpath, which follows the River Coln closely, but more directly across the bends; sometimes on higher ground to avoid flooding when the river 'comes out'. Aim for the middle of a conifer woodland ahead and enter it.

Bibury and the River Coln.

Inside it, many trees are deciduous, suggesting that the conifers on the outside edge were planted as protection for the deciduous trees.

From the woodland, follow the edge of its extension, bringing you closer to the river and its meandering course (and crossing the line of Akeman Street again). Cross two fields and enter Ash Copse (not many ashes at the time of writing).

Cross another field and go into Oxhill Wood, the track ascending the higher side of the wood, with the river almost completely concealed. A track from the left joins this one. At the next junction of tracks, bear right, downhill, out of the woodland, with a view of the valley and the house at Bibury Mill built of gleaming Cotswold stone.

The track winds its way down through the farm to the mill itself and out across the river. To the left is Bibury Court, now a hotel but once the home of the Sackville family. At the road, turn left, and left again, not down the road to the Court, but through the stone wall, to pass in front of village houses and down to the church gate.

The porch entrance in on the far side. The rear of Bibury Court overlooks the array of tombstones in the churchyard. From the church gate, bear left along the road, past the Village Hall, to join the footway beside the main road, and return to the start along the main road beside the river.

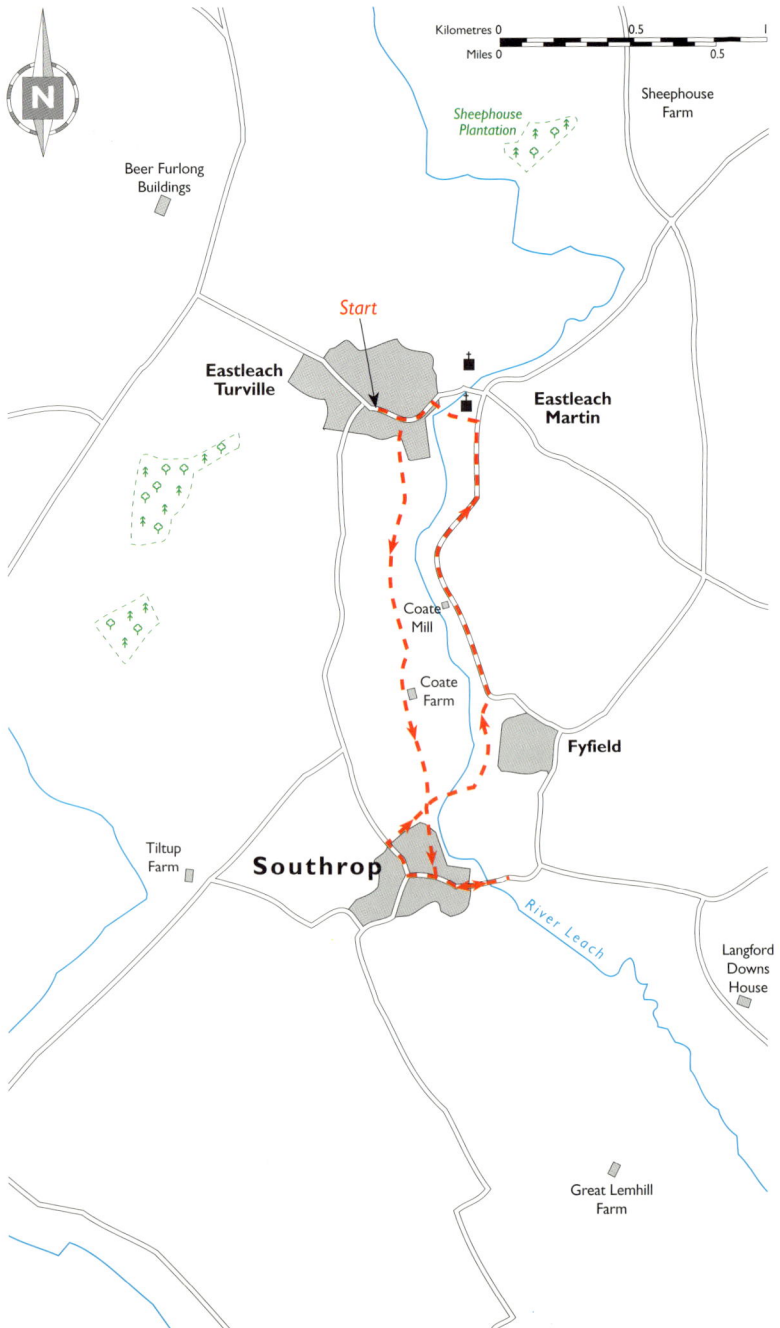

N

Kilometres 0   0.5   1
Miles 0   0.5

Sheephouse Farm

Sheephouse Plantation

Beer Furlong Buildings

Start

Eastleach Turville

Eastleach Martin

Coate Mill

Coate Farm

Fyfield

Tiltup Farm

Southrop

River Leach

Langford Downs House

Great Lemhill Farm

EASTLEACH

Eastleach is on the eastern edges of the Cotswolds as they merge with the Thames valley. The River Leach is a tributary of the Thames. It rises at the village of Hampnett, north-west of Northleach, and joins the Thames south-east of Lechlade. In places on its way it disappears below ground in summer, reappearing with the winter rains.

Eastleach Turville almshouses.

Walk along the upper road to the almshouses, turning right down a walkway to the lower road. Bear left and then right up a road, which bears right. Turn right at an electric pole, then just beyond the cottage turn left. The path is enclosed up to a stile. Straight ahead is another stile. In the next field, bear gently right above the river to converge on the wall on the ridge above.

The river meanders closer to you while the straighter mill race serves Coate Mill on the far side. Cross the next stile and aim for the house ahead. Cross a footbridge and bear right to a wicket gate. Turn left along the wall to pass the house, called Coate Farm.

Cross the drive and walk ahead in the next field, aiming for the stile between the line of the wall and trees. The hamlet of Fyfield is to the left. Further eastwards is RAF Brize Norton, and aircraft from there are frequently seen, and heard, in these skies.

Follow the fence on your left beside a new plantation. To your right is a large house with nesting holes for

INFORMATION

Distance: 5 km (3 miles).

Start and finish: Near Victoria Inn. Park considerably. Eastleach is 6 km north-east of Fairford, from the A417 Cirencester-Lechlade road, then minor roads. From the A40 at Burford, take minor roads south-west through Westwell.

Public transport: None currently available.

Terrain: Easy field walking, but can be muddy. Boots recommended in wet conditions.

Time: Allow 2 hours.

Refreshments: Eastleach: Victoria Inn. Southrop: Swan Inn.

doves in the wall. Continue ahead into Southrop, beside a strip of recently planted trees, aiming for a stone stile between cottages. Continue to the road, and turn left for a saunter along the street to the river.

Water gardens on the river Leach at Southrop.

From the river retrace your steps, passing the entrance to the Manor House (now on your left). Beyond it, on your left, is the entry to St Peter's Church, a simple Norman church with Saxon herringbone masonry in the nave, and an outstanding font representing Moses with the Ten Commandments and the Virtues trampling their corresponding vices.

John Keble, who was born in nearby Fairford, was curate here from 1823–25. During his time at the Vicarage he hosted many discussions amongst those who formed the religious Oxford Movement. Later, his name was given to an Oxford college. Another Oxford college connection is Dorothy Wadham, who bought the manor house and lands in 1612 and presented it to the college which she founded and which bears her name. It remained in the college's possession until sold in 1926.

Return to the road, turn left to the Swan inn, and turn right beside the green. Although tranquil now, this was the scene of a farm workers' riot in 1830. Poverty drove them to desperate measures and the riot in Southrop was dispersed by mounted militia with drawn sabres.

Follow the Eastleach road, and turn right again on a track. At the next field, the path aims half left towards

Fyfield (crossing the route on which you came to Southrop), and a bridge over the river. Turn left and walk beside the gently flowing Leach. Sluice gates suggest the use of the land for water meadows. The ground was flooded in early springtime to produce grazing as early as possible.

The path leaves the river to join the road. Turn left. Pass beside Coate Mill and follow the road north to Eastleach Martin. Turn left into the grounds of the Church of St Michael and St Martin, an unusual twin dedication. It dates from Norman times, being founded by Richard Fitzpons who took over the land following the Conquest. Sadly, it is now redundant. The costs of repair are borne by the Redundant Churches Fund, set up in 1969 to maintain outstanding churches no longer required for worship.

The Kebble clapper bridge joining Eastleach Turville and Eastleach Martin.

Beyond the church, go through a gate in the churchyard wall and turn left on the path beside the river. Springtime brings a mass of daffodils – and visitors to admire them. Cross the stone clapper bridge, called Keble's Bridge (he was curate here, too, but it may be named after other family connections). At the road, turn right if you wish to visit St Andrew's Church, with its saddleback roofed tower; or turn left, past the war memorial and along the major road to return to the Victoria Inn.

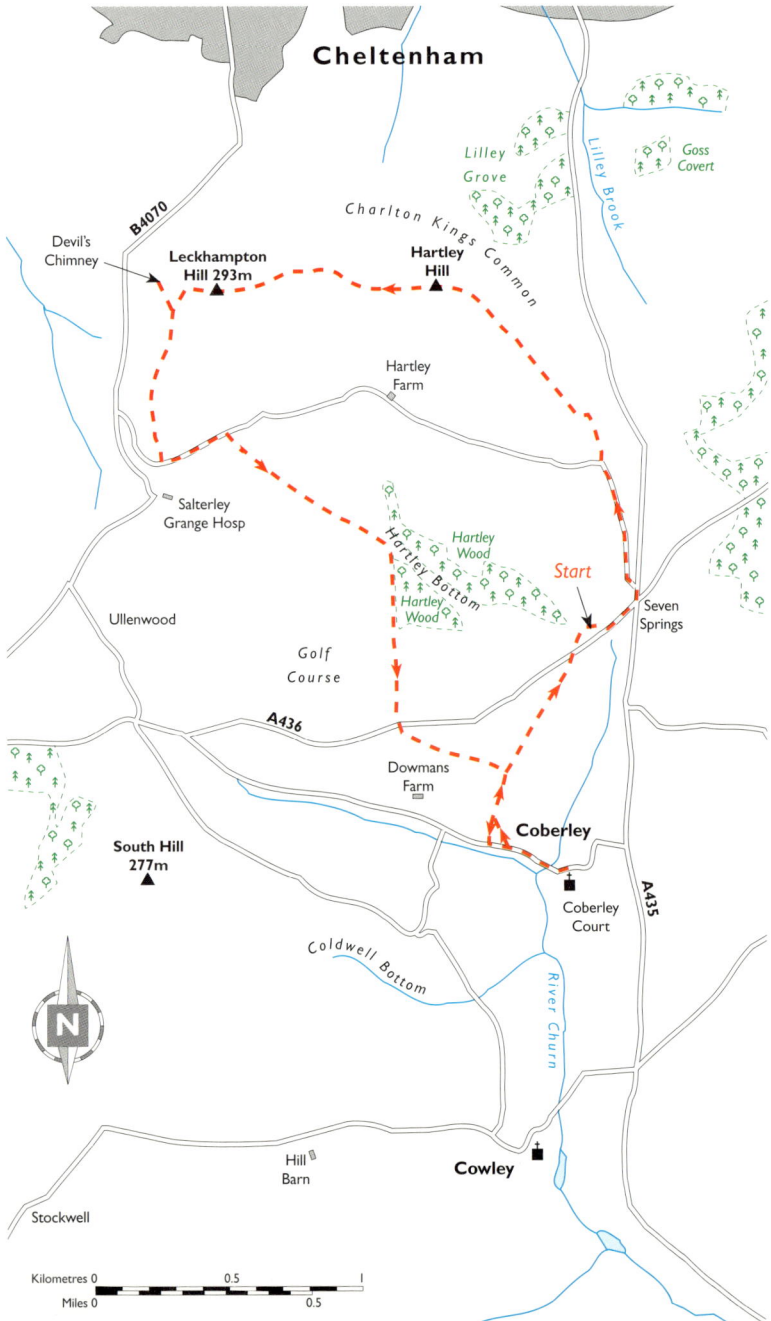

Cheltenham

B4070

Devil's
Chimney

Leckhampton
Hill 293m

Hartley
Hill

Lilley
Grove

Goss
Covert

Lilley Brook

Charlton Kings Common

Hartley
Farm

Salterley
Grange Hosp

Hartley
Wood

Hartley Bottom

Hartley
Wood

Start

Seven
Springs

Ullenwood

Golf
Course

A436

Dowmans
Farm

Coberley

South Hill
277m

Coberley
Court

A435

Coldwell Bottom

River Churn

N

Hill
Barn

Cowley

Stockwell

Kilometres 0   0.5   1
Miles 0   0.5

SEVEN SPRINGS

The Seven Springs, each emerging into a pool below the parking place, form the source of the River Churn, which joins the Thames at Cricklade. It is also the remotest source of the Thames, and therefore claims to be its true source. Hence the plaque on the wall above the exit from the pool proclaiming 'HIC TUUS O TAMESINE PATER SEPTEMGEMINUS FONS' ('Here, O Father Thames, your sevenfold source'). A mile to the north is the Cotswold scarp, the watershed between Thames and Severn. The walk returns to an attractive village with associations with Dick Whittington, Lord Mayor of London in medieval times.

Walk up the footway on the left to the junction of the A436 and A435 roads. Pass an AA telephone box and enter a lane on the left. The route follows the Cotswold Way for 5 km.

Source of the Rver Churn—the remotest source of the Thames.

Pass Windmill Farm and its defunct windpumps. Where the lane turns sharp left, continue ahead on a track. Turn left into a field and right along its top edge. The scrub of Charlton Kings Common comes into view ahead and is soon reached.

Along the scarp edge are a number of seats for viewing the Severn vale and the northern scarp. Follow the Cotswold Way onto a bridleway (blue arrows). The path rises through the gorse scrub ('when gorse is out of flower, kissing's out of season') towards the fence

INFORMATION

Distance: 10 km (6 miles).

Start and finish: Park opposite the Seven Springs Inn, on the old road at Seven Springs, on A436 (Gloucester-Andoversford) near to (and west of) junction with A435 (Cheltenham-Cirencester).

Public transport: Stagecoach from either Cheltenham or Swindon/Cirencester.

Terrain: Gentle rise to scarp edge. Field walking. Expect mud. Boots or strong shoes recommended.

Time: Allow 3–4 hours.

Refreshments: Seven Springs Inn, opposite parking place.

boundary on the left and past two bridleway gates. Follow the track through an embankment which forms the ramparts of the iron age hill fort on Leckhampton Hill. Bear right and head for the scarp edge at a topograph indicating the places to be seen from this point.

Continue southwards with the vale on your right. At a tall post with a waymark, turn very sharply right to follow a path (below the one you were on) to the Devil's Chimney, a rock thought to have been a relic of quarrying. These extensive quarries were served by a tramway to take the stone down for the building of Cheltenham. Retrace your steps to the tall post and follow the path beside the wall. Just before leaving Leckhampton Hill the path passes above Salterley quarry, now a car park.

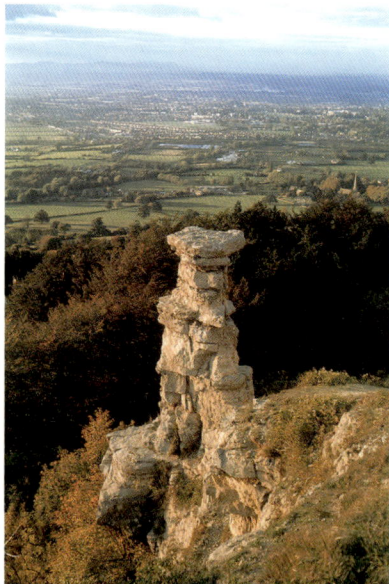

The "Devil's Chimney" rising above old quarries on Leckhampton Hill.

Turn left, uphill. Before the cottages, turn right into a track. Within a few steps, leave the track (and the Cotswold Way) by bearing left beside a wall, then a hedge, to a stile in a wire fence. Go down the slope beyond to a track below an electricity pylon. Turn right, following the valley bottom with the fence on your left (ignoring gates and stile in it). Follow up through a gate, into a field. At the end the path enters an enclosed track beside the golf course.

Carefully cross the road. Turn left and then right onto a footpath signed 'Coberley 0.5 km'. Strike out across the field half left to meet the corner of another field on the right. Follow this hedgeline ahead to a T-junction with a bridleway.

Turn right into the village of Coberley. Pass the school before reaching the village green. Past the village cross on your right, bear right onto a narrow footpath to the left of a house down to a road (near the village Post Office).

Turn left for 300 m to see the church, which is detached from the main settlement. It lies behind the frontage of Coberley Court, and access is through a sturdy wooden door. The entrance porch is on the far side. The nave and ceiling were restored through the generosity of a Coberly from Los Angeles, and a list in the porch shows how many friends the village has overseas, many with the name of this place, sometimes spelt in different ways. The local pronunciation is 'Cubberley' and this is the name often appearing in old maps and documents.

Sir Thomas Berkeley fought at the Battle of Crecy in 1346. His widow became the wife of Sir William Whittington and thus the mother of Sir Richard, the famous three-times Lord Mayor of London (in 1397, 1406 and 1419). Sir Thomas and Lady Berkeley/ Whittington are commemorated with effigies in a side chapel.

Return to the road and turn left to the village, bearing right on the road to the village green. Turn right at the top, leave the school and the houses on your left and enter the bridleway signposted 'Seven Springs 1 km'. Following the track with a hedge on your right, return to the T-junction mentioned earlier, and beyond, where the track turns left, turn right over a stile and onto a path across the field. This leads to the main road. Turn right and cross the road (again with care) to the parking area above the Seven Springs.

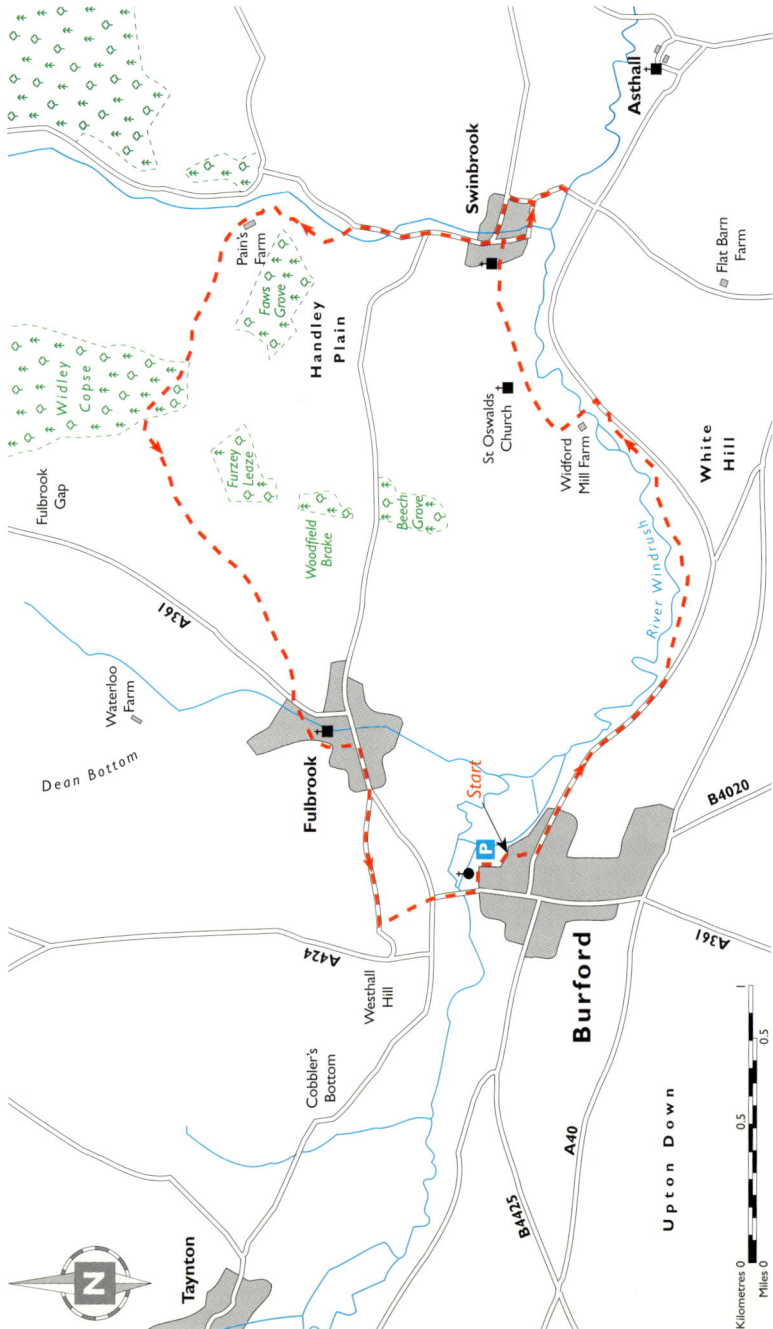

Asthall

Swinbrook

Flat Barn Farm

Pain's Farm

Faws Grove

Handley Plain

Widley Copse

St Oswalds Church

Fuzzey Leaze

Widford Mill Farm

White Hill

Fulbrook Gap

Woodfield Brake

Beech Grove

River Windrush

Waterloo Farm

Dean Bottom

Fulbrook

A361

Start

B4020

Burford

A424

Westhall Hill

A361

A40

B4425

Cobbler's Bottom

Upton Down

Taynton

Kilometres 0
Miles 0
0.5
0.5
1

BURFORD AND THE WINDRUSH

Burford, an Oxfordshire Cotswold town set on the southern slopes of the Windrush valley, is the 'borough on the ford', later replaced with a bridge, crossed at the end of the walk. Burford is well worth exploring; its attractions include the Cotswold garden behind *The Countryman* magazine's offices in Sheep Street, the Tolsey Museum, and the church. Cynthia Harnett's story for children (of all ages!) called *The Woolpack* is centred on the wool trade in Burford.

From the Guildenford car park turn left up Guildenford, admiring Cotswold domestic architecture and idyllic country cottage gardens. Turn left again along Witney Street, the original main road before the construction of what is now the A40. Follow the footway and then the road to a signpost for a footpath in the field on the left.

The path follows the Windrush downstream, taking a straighter course than the river, which lives up to its name ('winding amongst the rushes'). Riverside trees such as willow and alder abound. After several fields, the path rises to the road. Turn left and left again at Widford Mill Farm.

Over the river, turn right into a field above Widford Pool. The track follows the valley. To the left is the isolated chapel of St Oswald's, built on the foundations of a Roman villa. The chapel, usually open to the public (mind the well-worn step!), used to

INFORMATION

Distance: 10 km (6 miles).

Start and finish: Guildenford car park off Church Lane/ Guildenford. Burford is just north of the A40 on the A361 Swindon-Chipping Norton road.

Public transport: Swanbrook services from Cheltenham and Oxford. Walk down Main Street and turn into Church Lane, to reach car park entry.

Terrain: Easy field walking, but prepare for mud. Boots or strong shoes recommended.

Time: Allow 3–4 hours.

Refreshments: Burford: Inns and cafes in the town. Swinbrook: Swan Inn.

Toilets: Burford.

Opening hours: *Tolsey Museum:* end Mar-end Oct, daily, afternoons. May be open at other times – enquire locally.

The isolated chapel of St. Oswald in the fields at Widford.

be part of the long deserted medieval village of Widford ('willows by the ford').

The track continues ahead, passing to the left of a house, through three fields in which can be seen some terracing – all that remains of the Fettiplace family mansion. Built in Tudor times, it was eventually demolished in 1806. Astonishingly, no record of its appearance remains. The Fettiplace family line died out and in the 18th century the house was let to a Mr Freeman, an apparently respectable gentleman from London. However, he was arrested for highway robbery not far away. Swinbrook was a good retreat when London became too hot, perhaps.

The village of Swinbrook.

Beyond the stone walls ahead, the path is walled. Turn sharp left by the cottages to enter the churchyard. The Fettiplace tombs in the church illustrate interesting changes in style – formal in the 17th century, more relaxed in the 18th. Seats in the chancel, probably from Burford Priory at the time of the Dissolution, have interesting misericords.

Leaving the church porch, turn left, and onto the right hand path going down the steps beneath the lantern. Turn right, following the road down to the Swan Inn. The Windrush is bridged here also. Return towards the village, but turn right into the lane past 'The Old Farm'. At the road junction turn left down the hill, then turn right. A plank bridge saves wet feet at the ford.

Turn right on the road above, keeping right at the next junction. Before reaching more cottages, turn left into a small field, usually full of wild flowers in summer. Cross the stream, ascending the slope to cross a stile, and follow the right-hand hedgeline in the field above.

Turn right on the track and left at the next lane, which rises past the buildings of Pain's Farm and its cottages. The tarmac then deteriorates and the surface is made of Cotswold stone – perhaps looking like many Cotswold roads of 70 and 80 years ago.

On the left-hand track, enter the mixed woodland of Widley Copse. At the end of the woodland, turn left across the middle of three fields. If the farmer has continued recent tradition, your path will be cleared to a metre's width or more and you can delight in walking through a crop without fear of trespassing or causing damage.

Burford Church.

In the third field, the path converges on the hedgeline. Follow this to the right, finally dipping down to the left to reach the road at Fulbrook. Follow the left-hand verge, carefully crossing to the opposite side just before turning right down Upper End. Just beyond the garden on the left, enter the field. Aim to the right of Fulbrook church tower on the skyline. Cross a stile and then a stone stile to enter the churchyard.

The church is a 900-year-old Norman replacement for an earlier Saxon church. For nearly 400 years before the Reformation, the living was controlled by the Abbot of Keynsham. The massive yew tree outside the porch is estimated to be a thousand years old, perhaps as old as the church itself.

Leave the churchyard by the gates into Church Lane, to reach the main road and the village centre. Turn right, following the footway and grass verges. The Carpenter's Arms and the Mason's Arms perhaps indicate what a practical, working village this was. Turn right to Westhall Hill. Burford is seen on the left.

Westhall Hill is a delightful group of buildings ranging from the 16th to19th centuries. Just before reaching them, there is a barn/garage on the left; turn left on the path beside it. Bear left across the field into an enclosed path. Then descend the steps to the road. Cross carefully and follow the left-hand footway. Pass over the bridge at the foot of the town. The triangular insets in the parapet, originally designed to save people being run down by horses and carts, serve a similar purpose today!

To regain the car park, walk up the street to Church Lane and turn left.

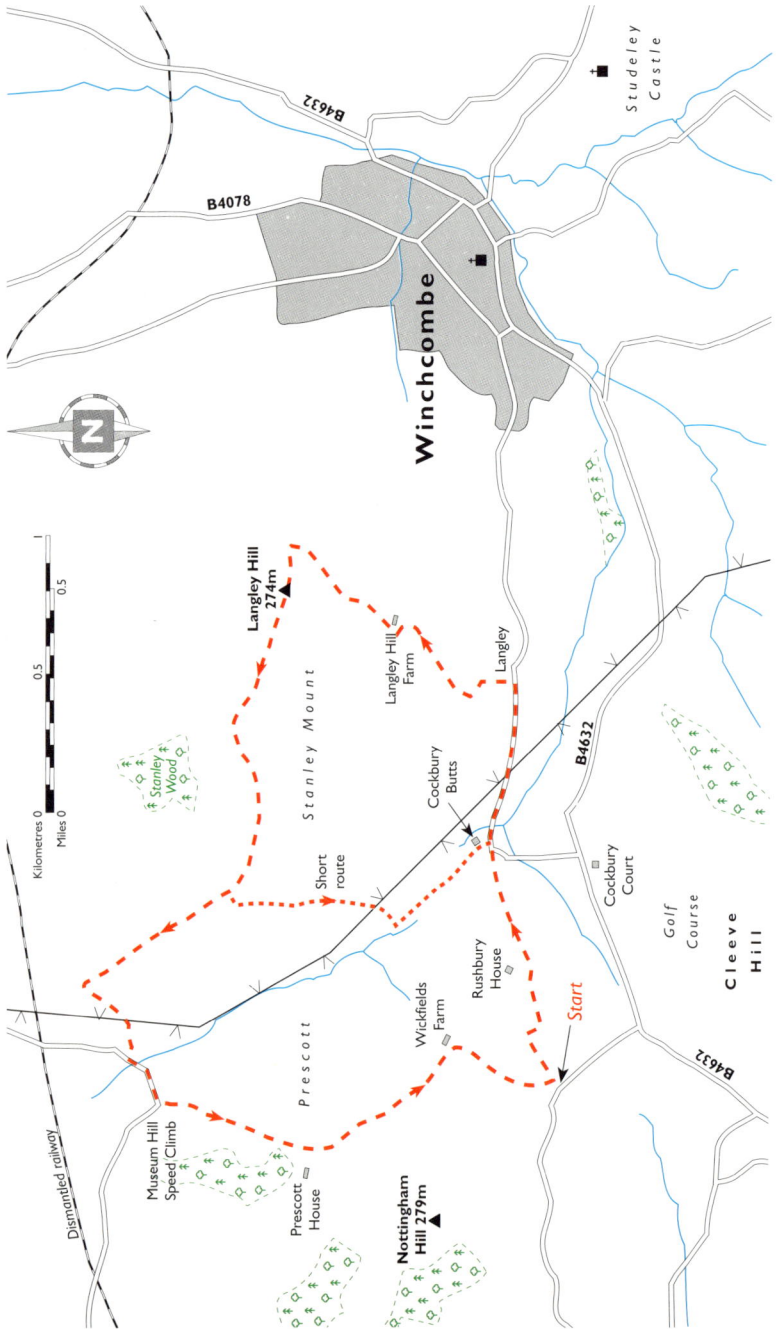

B4632

B4078

Winchcombe

Studeley Castle

Langley Hill 274m

Langley Hill Farm

Stanley Mount

Stanley Wood

Langley

Cockbury Butts

B4632

Short route

Cockbury Court

Golf Course

Rushbury House

Cleeve Hill

Prescott

Wickfields Farm

Start

B4632

Museum Hill Speed Climb

Prescott House

Nottingham Hill 279m

Dismantled railway

Kilometres 0   0.5   1

Miles 0   0.5

NORTH COTSWOLD OUTLIERS

'Outliers' are hills with the same underlying geology as the main mass but detatched from it. They are thought to have 'slipped' away from the main mass into the vale over millions of years, with the gaps between eroded by the action of water and rivers. This walk takes you over two outliers, with views of five others.

Walking from the B4632, turn right at the track junction over a stone stile. Follow the left-hand wall, turning right at the corner to cross a stile halfway along the next wall. Bear half right (with a view of Winchcombe church ahead) to the right of a cottage. Over the stile, descend to another by a barn. Cross the lane to pass through a gate. Bear half left down four fields, to a road seen near the cottage (Cockbury Butts) at the bottom.

Follow the road ahead for 900 m to Langley (the long 'leah' or woodland clearing). After passing two entrance drives (the second with pillars), turn left to follow a waymarked bridleway. Turning sharp right through a gate, ascend across three fields to Langley Hill Farm (views over Winchcombe to the right). In the last field, follow the left-hand fence up to a gate, and turn left. A wall of old railway sleepers contains silage (winter feed) covered with plastic weighted down with old tyres – interesting ways of recycling material.

Winchcombe lies in the valley between the outlier of Langley Hill and the main scarp.

INFORMATION

Distance: Full walk – 9 km (6 miles). Short walk – 7 km (4.5 miles).

Start and finish: Wickfields Lane, reached from B4632 Cheltenham-Winchcombe road. Turn off at the brow of the hill into a lane opposite the one signed 'Municipal Golf Course'. Park on rough ground beside the lane, and walk further to a track junction.

Public transport: Castleways Cheltenham to Winchcombe bus; alight at 'Municipal Golf Course' turn, but follow lane opposite instead. Walk to track junction.

Terrain: Gentle climbing and field walking. Expect mud, particularly on bridleways and in winter. Boots or strong shoes recommended.

Time: Full walk – allow 3–4 hours. Short walk – allow 3 hours.

Refreshments and toilets: None on route. Nearest are at clubhouse at Municipal Golf Course.

Opening hours: Bugatti Trust at Prescott Speed Hill Climb: Mon-Fri 1030–1530, admission free.

Turn right, opposite the silage clamp, passing through a gateway. If it is closed with electric wire, use the insulated handle for safe opening. This farm uses electric fencing extensively for flexible management of its enclosures and tracks. You may meet 'electric gates' at other points. Although not harmful, the shock can be unpleasant.

Passing through another gate, continue ahead into an old quarry area. Follow the sunken track to another carrying the Wychavon Way (which runs between Winchcombe and the River Severn near Droitwich). Turn left along the Wychavon Way, ignore the right-hand track, and enter a pasture field. The view over the vale shows other outliers – Bredon and Dumbleton Hills and, to the right of the flat vale of Evesham, Meon Hill at the end of the Cotswold range.

Turn left to follow the track for 400 m. At a waymark post, leave the Wychavon Way and bear left above the ruins of Warren Lodge Farm (so ruined it may be invisible in summer growth). Passing through a gateway, continue ahead across an undulating field. Ignore the footpath bearing left up the hill, but keep fairly close to the upper edge of the field to reach a ladder stile beside a gate.

The outliers of Woolstone and Dixton Hills.

Beyond is the next outlier, Prescott Hill. The path converges on a bridleway. The Knolls and Dixton Hill (with its flat-topped hill fort) are seen half left. Bear right down to the left-hand corner. Go through a gate.

For the short walk, go through a gate ahead, following an upper track bearing left through trees, emerging into a field and down to a gate. A half rearward look shows the Malverns closing the valley view, almost looking as if the Cotswolds go that far. Follow the left-hand edge and go through another gate. Turn right below the electricity pylon and follow the right-hand fence as it bears around the field to the left (ignore the gate on the right).

Bear left to follow woodland edge on the right, up to and around a reservoir to reach a rough track. This leads through three gates back to Cockbury Butts. Return to the start up the fields on the right used on the outward journey.

For the full walk, turn right to continue downhill on the same line as before. By a barn, turn right through a gate; follow a gully down through two bridlegates, bearing left to a third above a farmhouse. Turn left on the track, which then bears right. Keep straight ahead through a field gate, continuing across three fields to the road.

Turn left, using the right-hand verge. Before the next building, cross the road carefully to the left-hand verge to enter Prescott ('priest's cottage'). The thatched cottage at the road junction looks idyllically ancient, but is in fact a skilful restoration after a fire some years ago. The famous Prescott Hill Climb motor circuit is across the lane. Beyond its entrance, the Bugatti Trust has a museum open to the public.

The Bugatti Museum next to the Prescott Speed Hill Climb tells the story of Ettore Bugatti's inventions as well as cars such as this.

Turn left up the lane by the cottage. At the left turn, continue ahead on the rough track (tarred further up as the return route for vehicles on the Hill Climb). At Prescott House, turn left up the track through the woodland.

Emerging into fields, the track bears left, converging on a bridleway. Pass through a gate, and then white gates, into the grounds of Wickfields Farm. Through the farm, and holiday cottages, the road turns right, below the ramparts of Nottingham Hill hill fort, to the junction at the start.

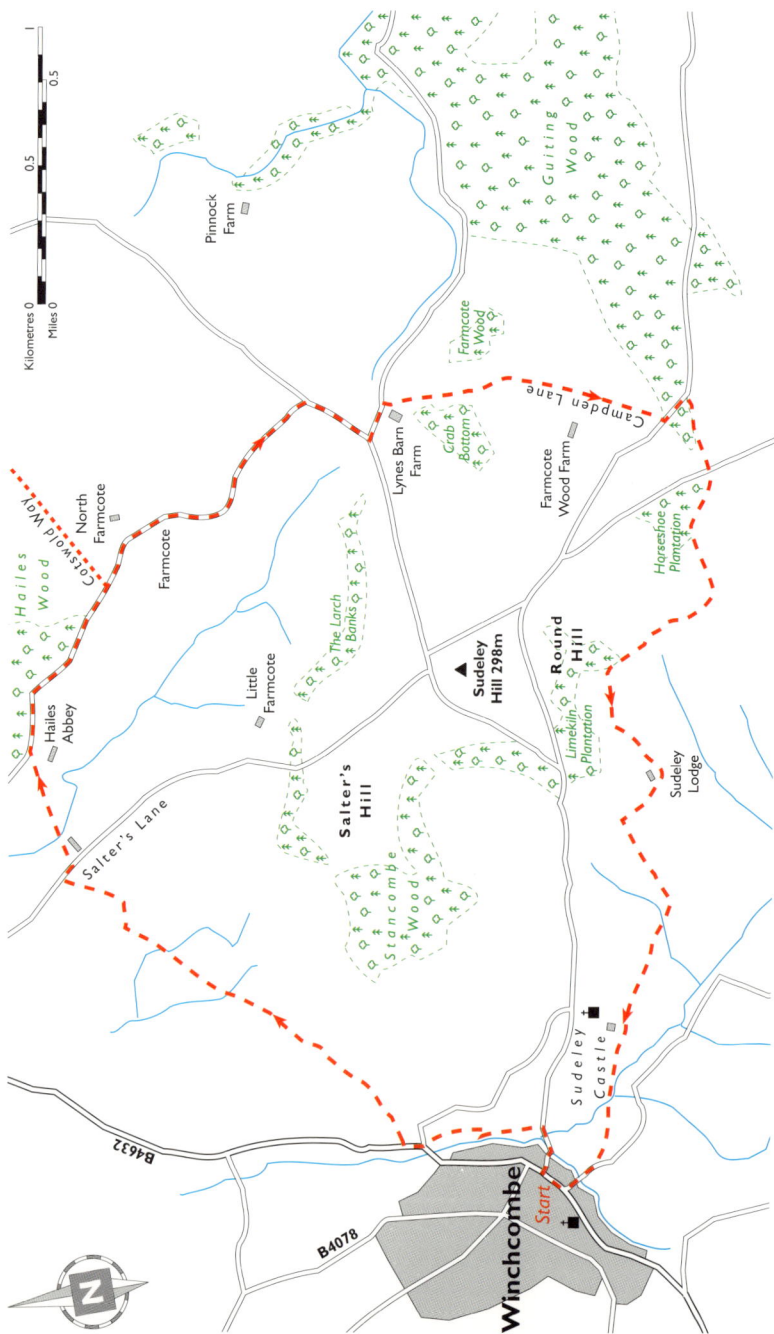

Kilometres 0
Miles 0

Pinnock Farm

Guiting Wood

Farmcote Wood

Campden Lane

Crab Bottom

Lynes Barn Farm

Farmcote Wood Farm

North Farmcote

Hailes Wood

Cotswold Way

Farmcote

Horseshoe Plantation

The Larch Banks

Little Farmcote

▲ Sudeley Hill 298m

Round Hill

Hailes Abbey

Salter's Lane

Salter's Hill

Limekiln Plantation

Sudeley Lodge

Stancombe Wood

B4632

Sudeley Castle

B4078

Winchcombe

Start

N

WINCHCOMBE AND HAILES

Winchcombe, 'corner of the valley', was a regional capital of the kingdom of Mercia before the Conquest in 1066. Winchcombe Abbey was above Abbey Terrace behind the high wall. Nothing remains above ground; the stone would have been carried away for use elsewhere – easier than quarrying fresh stone.

The parish church is next to the Abbey site, and dates from the 1460s. It has interesting gargoyles outside, said to be the masons' way of poking fun at local worthies. Inside is a late 19th century east window representing St Peter, to whom the church is dedicated, walking on the water. A Tudor oak screen, previously between choir and nave, is beautifully carved and careful examination will reveal the face of

River Isbourne on its way to join the Avon.

INFORMATION

Distance: 11 km (7 miles).

Start and finish: Winchcombe Abbey Terrace. Park here or behind the library in Back Lane and walk along Cowl Street to Abbey Terrace.

Public transport: Castleways: Cheltenham-Winchcombe-Broadway bus. Alight at Abbey Terrace.

Terrain: Easy field walking, and gentle climbs. Expect mud. Boots or strong shoes recommended.

Time: Allow 4 hours.

Refreshments: Winchcombe: Inns and cafes in town. Hailes: Hayles Fruit Farm in season. Sudeley Castle.

Toilets: Winchcombe: junction of Abbey Terrace and Vineyard Street.

Opening hours: *Hailes Abbey (National Trust/English Heritage):* Apr-Oct, daily 1000–1800; Nov-Mar, Tue-Sun 1000–1600; admission charge includes audio tour (NT members free). *Sudeley Castle:* Apr-Oct, daily 1100–1700; admission charge.

an imp – presumably another touch of humour from the artisans.

Further west along the street is a new development named Tobacco Close. This commemorates the illegal growing of tobacco in the 17th century when the plantations in Virginia needed protection. The militia from Cheltenham dealt with that!

Walk northwards from Abbey Terrace towards Broadway. The street is flanked with 'black and white' half-timbered buildings. The George Inn is seen near the junction with North Street. It was a medieval hostelry with a courtyard and an external gallery to give access to the upper rooms. Opposite, on the corner of North Street, is the Town Hall with a set of stocks outside. You can muse on why there is an odd number of holes for feet!

For the walk, turn right down narrow Castle Street. Pass a lane, and cross the bridge over the river Isbourne. Opposite holiday cottages in old buildings of Sudeley Castle, turn left up an alley between the houses.

Beyond the gate, follow the bank above the river. To the left are the buildings of Hailes Street and Silk Mill Lane, cascading down to the river. To the right, the 'ridge and furrow' formation in the fields suggests cultivation for a thousand years.

The road bridge ahead has been widened from its original name of 'Footbridge'! For safety, cross the main road, turning right for 100 m. Re-cross to follow the Cotswold Way up Puck Pit Lane. This would have been the route from Winchcombe followed by Richard, Earl of Cornwall, and his brother, Henry III, to dedicate Hailes Abbey in 1251.

At the end, crossing the stile beside a gate, aim half left. Continue across the next field, with views widening over the Vale and the railway station at Greet. This Stratford-Cheltenham line, opened in 1905 and closed in the 1960s with the Beeching cuts, is being restored by a dedicated group of volunteers

from the Gloucestershire and Warwickshire Railway Society (GWR for short). Their base at Toddington is seen ahead.

Continue through a kissing gate (Didbrook church ahead), crossing to another. Cross the corner of the next field and over a stile. Walk diagonally to a white target in the hedge ahead (the path follows a long removed hedgeline, but the right of way stays until legally diverted). Turn right at the target, then left at the next track, and continue to a road junction.

Turn right for 300 m along part of the Saltway, an ancient route linking Droitwich in Worcestershire with the Thames at Lechlade. Turn left beside a cottage, pass through a field gate and cross to the far right-hand corner. Hailes Abbey ruins are on the right. The 12th century church on the left, built before the Abbey, contains medieval wall paintings.

The ruined cloisters of Hailes Abbey.

Not much of the Abbey remains apart from the ground level outlines of the walls. If you go in, take the excellent audio tape guide as you walk round. You will learn of Earl Richard's vow to build an abbey if he survived a stormy sea passage. He did, and in 1246 building started at Hailes.

Many pilgrims came to wonder at the relic of the Holy Blood, a phial said to have been preserved from the Crucifixion. This relic was declared a fraud at the Reformation, shortly before the monastery was dissolved.

Walk up the road past the Abbey to the entrance to Hayles Fruit Farm. Follow the Cotswold Way up the track. Where it turns left across the fields, continue upwards into the hamlet of Farmcote, a manor owned in the 14th century by the Stratford family, some of whom achieved high office in church and state.

St. Faith's at Farmcote.

Along the lane is St Faith's church, a simple chapel in the parish of Temple Guiting 3 km away. Follow the lane and turn right at the road junction. Turn left at the next junction.

Pass a cottage and a farm on the right. Turn right at a bridleway signpost, to follow part of Campden Lane, a prehistoric track. Aim for the left-hand edge of the woodland on the horizon. Passing a derelict house, keep to the left hedgeline beyond it. Above right is Farmcote Wood Farm, its woodland strategically placed to break the northerly wind. Pass through the edge of Guiting Wood and onto the road.

Turn left. Continue up the road (Wardens' Way joins here) to a clearing on the right. Turn right and right again, into a field beside a wall, largely outgrown by a hedge. The road beyond is the Saltway again. You can perhaps see in your mind's eye the pack horses carrying salt over the Cotswolds for loading into London-bound barges at Lechlade. Turn left for 50 m, before turning right onto a track.

The Wardens' Way guides you back to Winchcombe. The view is across the vale of the Severn with the Malverns as the backdrop.

Turn right above Parks Farm buildings, which provide an eye-level view of roofs made of Cotswold slate or 'slats'. They were quarried or mined. Sometimes they were split manually; sometimes the blocks were kept covered, their moisture splitting them when exposed to frost. Laying the largest at the eaves and smallest at the ridge ensured a lighter load on the frame and best use of all the stone. The 'slats' have different name according to size – cocks, cuttings, muffets, becks, bachelors, wivutts amongst them.

Follow the farm drive round the valley down to Sudeley Lodge and beyond to Sudeley Lodge Cottages on the right. Turn left, keeping to the right-hand boundary. Crossing the stile, turn right, near an oil pipeline marker, and left down to another stile. Bearing right on a rough track for 50 m, cross a stile and stone footbridge. Enter the Home Parks of Sudeley Castle. Waymarks across the field bring you to a gate beside the Castle.

Henry VIII's last wife, Katherine Parr, is buried here. The Castle was 'slighted' (fortifications destroyed) during the Civil War (mid 17th century) and was largely ruinous until the glove-making Dent family came in the 19th century to restore the Castle and provide facilities in Winchcombe, including a school and almshouses.

Walk ahead (adventure playground on the right), to a field gate, along the Castle drive, over the Beesmoor Brook and out of the grounds beside the Almsbury Lodge. From the bridge over the Isbourne, above the allotments, can be seen the Dent almshouses with characteristic red and cream stones over the windows and doors. They were designed in 1865 by Sir George Gilbert Scott, whose other works include the Albert Memorial and St Pancras Station in London.

Walk up Vineyard Street, once called Duck Street because of the ducking stool by the river for unruly wives! At the top is Abbey Terrace.

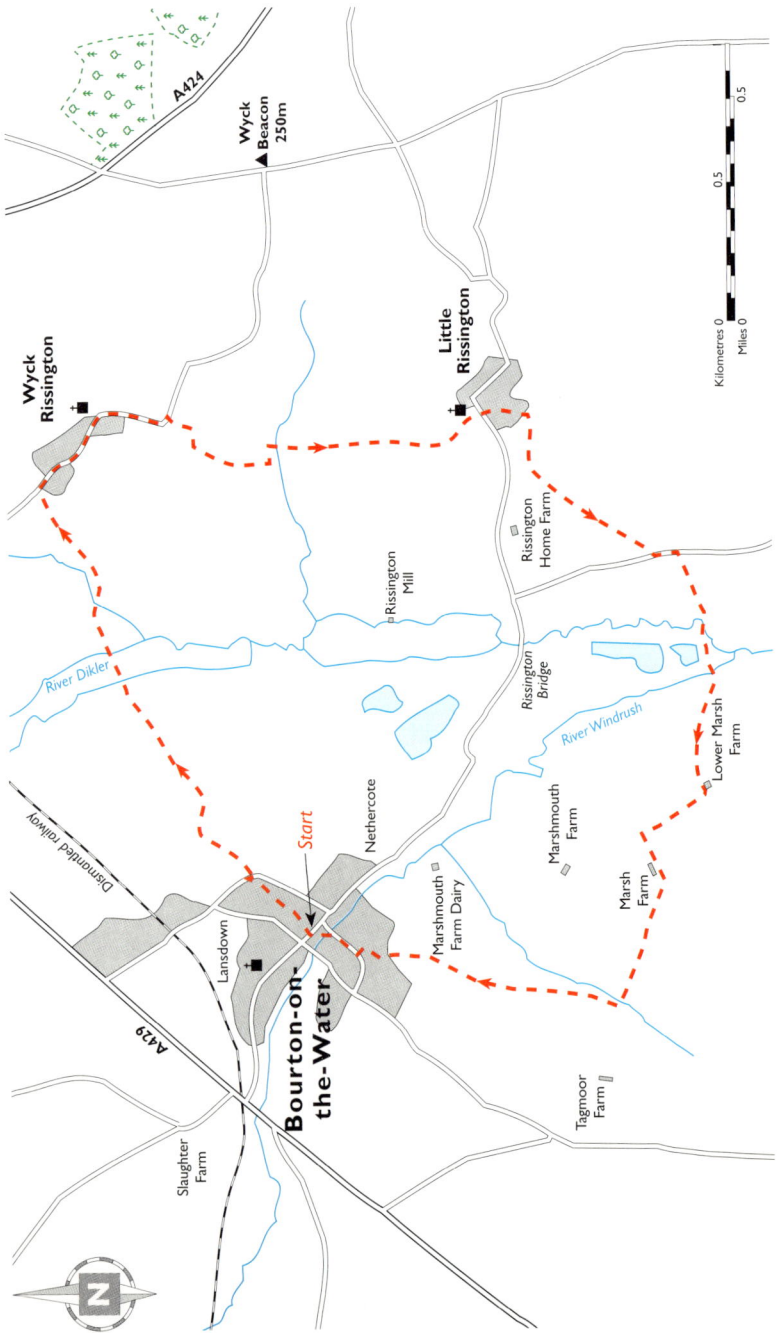

Wyck Beacon 250m ▲

A424

Wyck Rissington ✝ ■

Little Rissington ✝ ■

Rissington Home Farm

Rissington Mill

Rissington Bridge

River Dikler

River Windrush

Lower Marsh Farm

Marshmouth Farm

Marsh Farm

Nethercote

Start

Marshmouth Farm Dairy

Lansdown

Bourton-on-the-Water

Dismantled railway

A429

Slaughter Farm

Tagmoor Farm

Kilometres 0

Miles 0

0.5

0.5

0.5

N

BOURTON ON THE WATER

Bourton is close to the Roman Fosseway, but the iron age fort of Salmonsbury was there before them. Plenty of modern interests could delay your start. A model of the village of Bourton is in the grounds of the Old New Inn (with, of course, a model of the model in the grounds of the model . . .). The Model Railway Exhibition provides delight with its working layouts. The Motor Museum, in the old mill, is not only packed with memorabilia of motoring history but also includes some oddities such as a glass cruet in the shape of a car!

The Motor Museum is housed in the old mill on the River Windrush.

Near the Model Railway Exhibition is a lamp post with various sign arms. Several walking routes begin or end here – the Heart of England Way (from Cannock Chase), Wardens' Way and Windrush Way (to Winchcombe) and the Oxfordshire Way (to Henley on Thames). A fine choice for the long distance walker. Follow the Oxfordshire Way signs between the houses away from the road. Turn left and right, crossing Station Road car park, and continue beyond to the road. Turn right and left into a lane. Ignoring the steps by Woodlands House, walk a few yards further to steps up to a stile on the right.

Follow the left hand hedge. In the next field, bear diagonally up to the far right corner on the northern embankment of Salmonsbury camp. Follow the left hand hedge to a track. Cross over, following the Oxfordshire

INFORMATION

Distance: 10 km (6 miles).

Start and finish: Village centre near Model Railway Exhibition. Bourton is east of the A429, between Stow on the Wold and Northleach.

Car parking: Large car parks on Rissington Road and Station Road.

Public transport: Pulham's buses from Cheltenham, Stow on the Wold and Moreton in Marsh.

Terrain: Easy field walking, mostly level. No special footwear needed.

Time: Allow 3–4 hours.

Refreshments: Bourton on the Water: Inns, hotels and cafes.

Toilets: Behind Victoria Hall.

Opening hours: The many attractions in Bourton are generally open during normal hours, but may be restricted out of season.

Way to a bridle bridge, and to a bridlegate and footbridge over an area that is boggy in wet weather. Beyond is the River Dikler, where Wyck Mill stood, long vanished except for stonework beside the bridge you cross.

Bear slightly left over the rise, cross the next brook and turn left through three fields to the road at the west end of Wyck Rissington. Turn right along the road, flanked by the village green and rows of chestnuts, to the church. The house before the church used to be the rectory. In its garden, Canon Cheales constructed a maze as recently as the 1950s, now removed but commemorated in the church.

The road bears right, and where it turns left, walk ahead on a 'no through road' used as a farm track, through a number of gates until it becomes a grassy avenue between trees. At the end turn left to, and through, a gate. Ignore the bridleway (blue arrow) bearing away to the left and proceed straight ahead.

The path climbs ahead in the next field, and in the one beyond runs along an embankment giving excellent views from Stow on the Wold (behind you) to the village of Clapton on the Hill towards the skyline, half right. Follow the left-hand hedge in the next field, arriving at the church gates at Little Rissington. Many Cotswold churches were outposts of abbeys in the vales either side. St Peter's here was given to Osney Abbey near Oxford.

Modern headstones in Little Rissington's church yard commemorate airforce personnel who gave their lives to defend ours

A book in the church records all the graves in the churchyard. Not only does it show the major family names in the village over the centuries, but also the names of members of the Royal Air Force who died while stationed at the airfield above the village, plus members of the Royal Canadian, Australian and New Zealand Air Forces. That section of the churchyard is a smaller, but equally significant, version of the war cemeteries in many places worldwide.

From the church, walk down the path, through the gates and towards the village. If this seems a romantic place to get married, remember a local tradition requiring the groom to lift his bride over these gates!

Cross the road with care, into the lane opposite. At the end of the wall of the

Little Rissington Church is approached from the fields.

last house, turn right. Over the stile, and at the end of the left-hand fence, bear half left across the field to a gate. The path crosses the boundaries of three fields near the corners, and, in the fourth, strikes diagonally to a gate onto the road just above the far left corner.

Turn left. At the second gate on the right, turn right to follow the hedgeline. Turn right over the footbridge crossing the Dikler, and left following the path between the field and the river. Turn left into the next field, where the path runs near a lake resulting from gravel digging.

Left again, cross a stile, and right to cross the River Windrush by a footbridge. Follow the right-hand hedgeline through two fields to a farm track (stiles are equipped with sleeper walkways for wet weather). Continue ahead on the track and turn right on another. At a gateway turn left and walk through Marsh Farm. Beyond the left-hand gate, bear right to the hedgeline. Go through the gate (not the stile right of it). Follow the hedgeline, first on the right, and after a gate/stile, on the left. Turn left over a footbridge, and right beside the hedge. Walk to an opening to the left of the field corner (Tagmoor Farm is above, in front).

Turn right, diverging from the right-hand hedge, through three fields. The path then keeps to the right-hand hedge, but launches you across the field beyond to the middle of the hedgeline ahead. Crossing another footbridge, walk across to a gate by an enclosure. Follow the fence and then the building on the left, continuing ahead into a street. Turn left into Clapton Row then right (Victoria Street). Turn left and, just beyond the Victoria Hall, turn right over the river back to the starting lamp post.

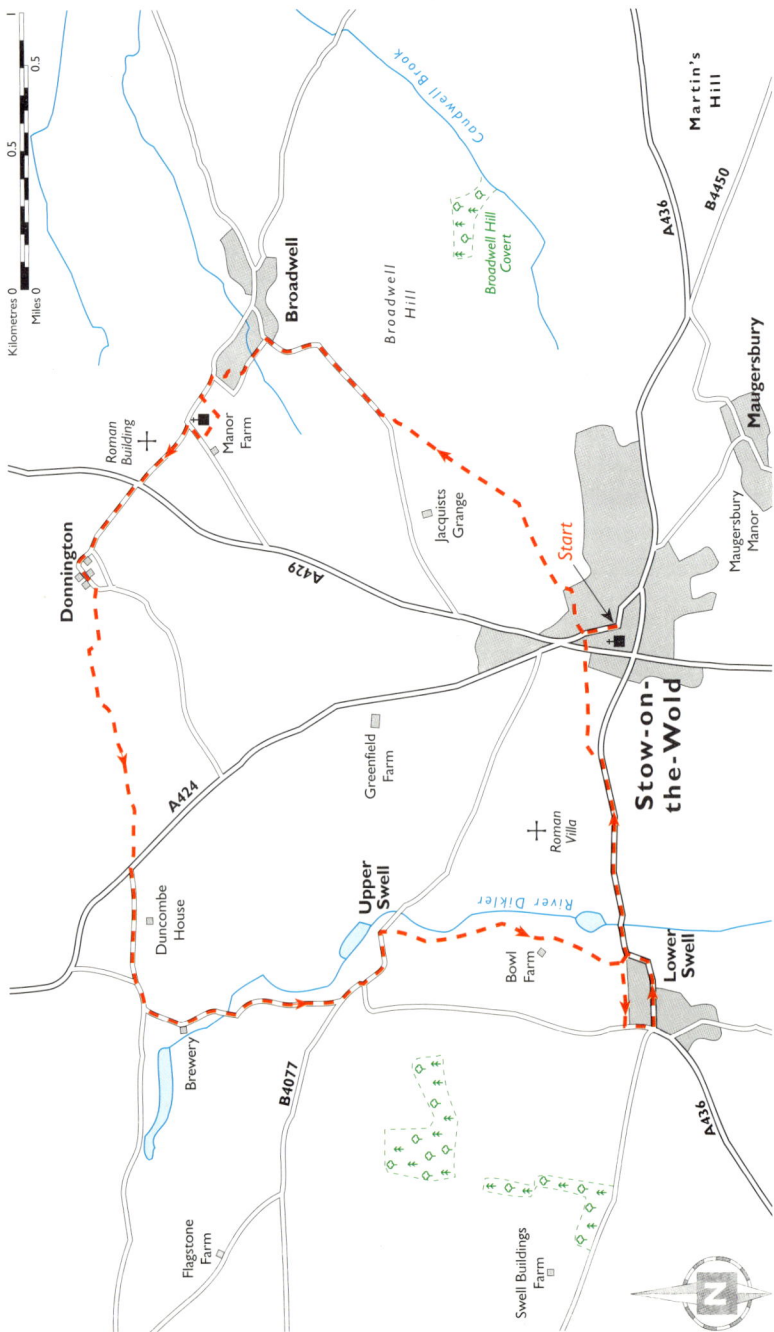

Kilometres 0
Miles 0

0.5

0.5

Coldwell Brook

Broadwell

Broadwell Hill Covert

Broadwell Hill

Martin's Hill

B4450

A436

Maugersbury

Maugersbury Manor

Roman Building

Manor Farm

Donnington

Jacquists Grange

A429

Start

Stow-on-the-Wold

A424

Greenfield Farm

Roman Villa

Duncombe House

Upper Swell

River Dikler

Bowl Farm

Lower Swell

Brewery

B4077

A436

Flagstone Farm

Swell Buildings Farm

STOW ON THE WOLD

'Stow on the Wold where the wind blows cold, and the cooks can't cook their dinners' – hardly surprising at about 230 m (750 ft) above sea level, on the top of a hill.

The church, founded by Evesham Abbey, has a thousand-year history with two substantial renovations, lastly in the 19th century. In 1646, at the close of the Civil War, the Battle of Stow actually took place near Donnington, but in the aftermath the streets of Stow flowed with blood and the Roundheads kept their Cavalier prisoners in the church.

Many roads converge on Stow, including the Fosse Way which marked the boundary of Roman Britain before later conquests. The town was a noted market centre for sheep, but later the Stow Fairs in May and October featured horses; these now take place at Andoversford, leaving the Stow events more of the fringe entertainment.

From St Edward's Hall, walk northwards (Moreton direction). Turn right into Parson's Corner, turning left along the road to Stow Well, one of the original water supplies for the town. Continue to a lodge house and bear left onto a track, giving wide views out to the Evenlode valley. Stow is on a ridge between the rivers Evenlode and Dikler.

At the road, turn right and walk into Broadwell. Turn left at the large green, passing the Fox Inn. Turn right beside the stream until it emerges at another, smaller green with a typical Cotswold bus shelter. Bear left on the road (signposted Donnington).

To visit the church, use the broad drive beside it and turn right into the churchyard. Originally 12th century, the church shows later work to the 19th century. The north door has a panel or tympanum above it of Norman origin, with a carved Maltese cross. There are round-topped wool bale tombs in the churchyard from the early 17th century. The path

INFORMATION

Distance: 11 km (7 miles).

Start and finish: St Edward's Hall (housing the library) in the Market Square.

Car parking: In or near the Square, or car park in Maugersbury road.

Public transport: Pulham's bus from Cheltenham.

Terrain: Easy rolling country, with some road walking. See note below. No special footwear needed.

Time: Allow 4 hours.

Refreshments: Stow on the Wold – Inns, hotels and tea rooms. Broadwell – Fox Inn. Lower Swell – Old Farmhouse Hotel, Golden Ball Inn.

Toilets: Stow – north end of Square, and Maugersbury road car park.

Note: Stow, a delightful town, is not well-served with footpaths radiating into the countryside around. Half of this walk is on the quieter country roads and lanes, with 1 km (0.6 mile) on major roads without a footway (though there is some verge). This should be considered if you have young children or dogs with you.

continues to the far wall of the churchyard; turn right to rejoin the route at another junction, again signposted Donnington.

Cross the Fosse Way and walk up the lane opposite. Where the major road bends left into Donnington village, bear right in front of some barns and turn left at the gateway to the Manor. At the next junction, turn right onto a footpath. At the second field on the left, turn left and follow the left-hand boundary to another stile, and to another. Bear half right, converging on the boundary below a power line. The Battle of Stow took place in the fields to the right. At the next field, bear half left down the slope. After a stile, turn right to meet the corner of a mature hedge coming from the right. Enter and follow an enclosed path (also carrying the Heart of England Way) to the road.

The brewery at Donnington.

Cross and continue on the lane opposite. Keep ahead at the first junction, turn left at the second. Down the hill on the right is Donnington Brewery (not open). Between the buildings is a glimpse of the lake, which would have provided power for its previous use as a mill for 500 years until it became a brewery in the 1860s. The buildings are of Cotswold stone, with Welsh blue slate roofs replacing Cotswold 'slats'. Donnington Ales are served in many Cotswold inns, and for those partial to the brew (and others), a local author has created a 'Donnington Way' walk which links them!

Continue to the B4077 road just outside Upper Swell. Bear left down the road, on the right-hand verge. Before the bridge, turn right into a field. Bear right over a stile, and ascend diagonally, crossing an intermediate stile, to the right-hand end of a fence ahead. (The writer found the owner's requested field edge route uncomfortably narrow, and recommends the above legal right of way.)

After three kissing gates on the field edges (with interesting semi-circular walls), walk ahead on the ridge with the river at the bottom of the field to the left. The path converges on a drive; follow this to a stile on the right just before the road at Lower Swell. 'Swell' means rising ground, and you have just traversed the edge of this between Upper and Lower Swell.

To explore Lower Swell, cross the stile on the right. Cross half right to the corner of a garden wall, following it to a stile and track to a road. The church, on the right, has an interesting finial representing the moon, and an open bell tower with three bells.

Turn left down the road, and left twice again, to follow the footway past the Hotel and the Inn. Passing an estate lodge house, turn right up the road to Stow.

Half left, there is a view of Abbotswood, remodelled by Sir Edwin Lutyens in the early 20th century. Further along the road are Spa Cottages. A chalybeate spring was discovered here in 1807, hence the name of the cottages. If its potential had been realised in the fashionable days of 'taking the waters', Lower Swell might have developed into a Cheltenham or Bath.

Spa Cottages in Lower Swell.

Use the verge beyond the footway. 50 m before a barn on the right, turn left into a field. Bear right, aiming for the end of the houses to the left of Stow church tower, passing the cricket field on the way. Enter a private road (public for walkers) to reach the Fosse Way again. Cross and follow the alley ahead back to the Square.

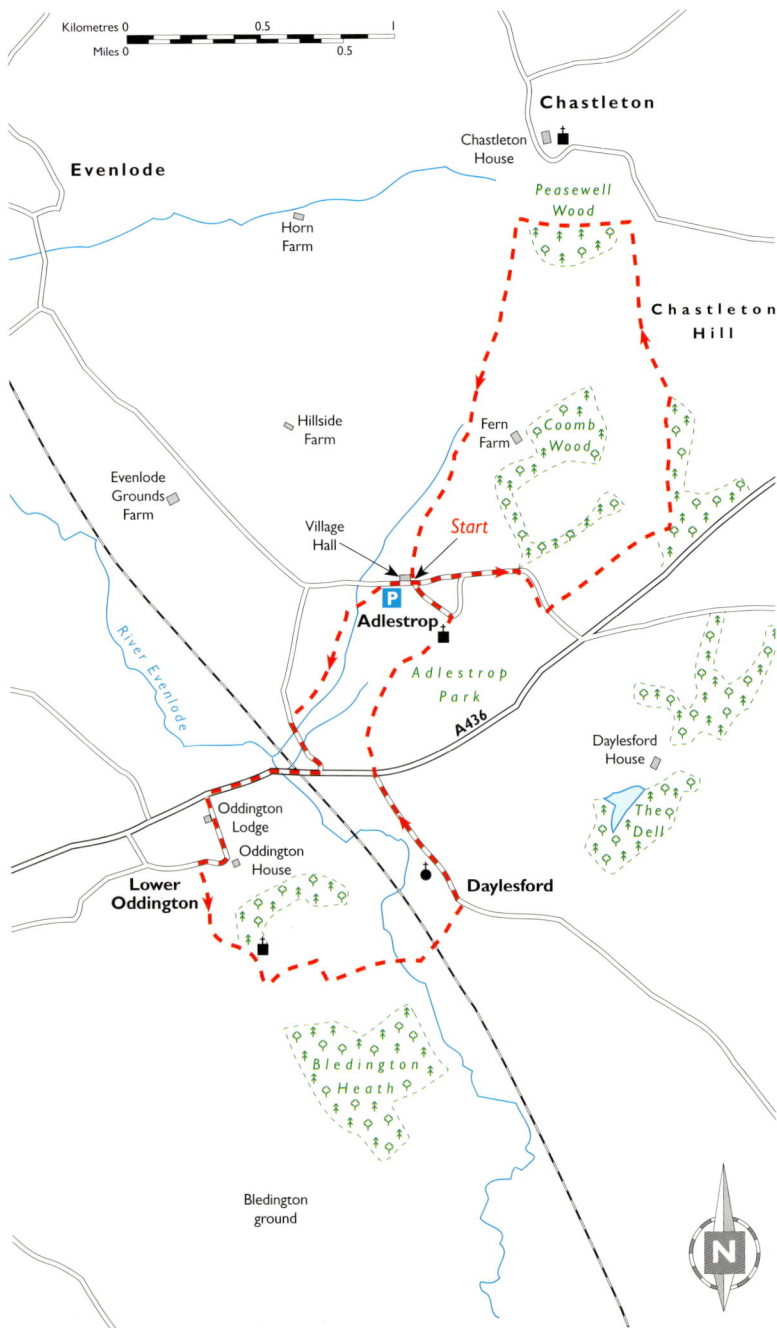

Kilometres 0   0.5   1
Miles 0   0.5

Chastleton

Chastleton
House

Evenlode

*Peasewell
Wood*

Horn
Farm

**Chastleton
Hill**

Hillside
Farm

Fern
Farm

*Coomb
Wood*

Evenlode
Grounds
Farm

Village
Hall

Start

P

Adlestrop

*Adlestrop
Park*

A436

Daylesford
House

*The
Dell*

Oddington
Lodge

Oddington
House

**Lower
Oddington**

Daylesford

River Evenlode

*Bledington
Heath*

Bledington
ground

N

ADLESTROP

s you come out of the car park you cannot miss the bus shelter to the left. The signboard came from the station, now defunct, and perhaps it would not have been rescued if Edward Thomas had not made Adlestrop famous with his poem, which you can read on the seat. That moment on the train preserving the golden days of the early 20th century contrasts with the shortness of his life.

He was killed in the First World War at the age of 39. Maybe you will be here on a day such as the one on which he came:

'And for that minute a blackbird sang
Close by, and round him, mistier,
Farther and farther, all the birds
Of Oxfordshire and Gloucestershire.'

Just over a hundred years earlier, Jane Austen was visiting her relatives here.

The first loop starts at the car park. Turn right on the road and after 150 m, beyond the houses, enter the field on the left over a stile and cross diagonally to the far left corner. Over the footbridge, follow the left-hand boundary in the next field. Young trees have been planted, and summer butterflies enjoy what we might call weeds. Again, Thomas summed up the scene:

'And willows, willow-herb and grass,
And meadowsweet, and haycocks dry,
Not whit less still and lonely fair
Than the high cloudlets in the sky.'

To the left, the Lodge of Adlestrop Park can be seen in front of the church at Daylesford.

Turn left at the road. The lake of the Adlestrop estate is on the left, and a poplar plantation on the right. Ignore the little road to the right. It was an access to the old station where Edward Thomas's train stopped 'unwontedly' on that day of high summer.

INFORMATION

Note: The walk described is a figure-of-eight. Either half can be walked, or both together.

Distance: First loop 6 km (4 miles); second loop: 5 km (3 miles).

Start and finish: Adlestrop Village Hall car park on northern edge of village. Donation requested. Adlestrop is north-east of Stow on the Wold, north of the A436; and south-west of Chipping Norton via A44 and A436.

Terrain: Gentle field and woodland walking. No special footwear needed.

Time: First loop: 2 hours plus; second loop: 2 hours.

Refreshments: Oddington (on first loop): Fox Inn.

Opening hours: *Chastleton House (National Trust):* Re-opening after restoration 1996/7. Enquire locally.

At the main road junction turn right and follow the footway over the railway line, which still links London, Oxford, Evesham and Worcester.

Turn left at the turn for Oddington. Walk through the village, passing the Fox Inn and going round to the right behind it. Turn left along the lane to the 11th century church of St Nicholas, standing on its own about 500 m beyond the present village. The village was abandoned and later rebuilt on its present location. Another church was built, and therefore this one languished until the early 20th century before being restored. The Doom painting on the north wall, representing the Last Judgement, would have been for the benefit of those who could not read, and there is a fine Jacobean pulpit.

Walk along the lane past the church for about 150 m, then turn left onto a footpath, following the headland path beside the hedge on the left and turning right at the corner. Where a hedge joins on the left, turn left to follow it on the bridleway beside it. At the end bear right and go over two bridges. Turn right after the

Daylesford village.

second to join the track which rises to cross the railway again (a red weight limit notice is a handy waymark). Beyond the bridge, follow the field boundary on the left to the road. Turn left and walk through Daylesford village.

In the churchyard are the graves of Warren Hastings and the Grisewood family. Hastings, born in 1732 not far away at Churchill (Walk 20) was the first

Governor General of India. On his retirement in 1784, he was impeached by Parliament for corruption but following a famous trial which dragged on for seven years and ruined Hastings financially, he was completely exonerated. Daylesford House, where he spent his last years until his death in 1818, is usually invisible in the trees. The Grisewoods were connected with the BBC. Freddy, a well known broadcaster over a long span of its first 60 years, grew up in the Rectory beside the church.

The road reaches the main A436 again. Cross over and enter the Park beside the Lodge, to follow the bridleway. This view would have been familiar to Jane Austen when visiting her cousin the rector, Rev Thomas Leigh, 200 years ago. The mansion, largely rebuilt in the 18th century, is across the parkland to the right. It is said that her stay here provided material for her novel Mansfield Park.

A street in Adlestrop.

The bridleway leads round to the right, past the cricket ground and into Adlestrop village by the church. Opposite the church is the old rectory, now Adlestrop House. The lane keeps left, passing the Post Office and more cottages (beflowered in summer) to reach the Village Hall.

The second loop leaves the car park and turns left following the major road up the hill (ignore the second turn into the village). As the road rises, turn into the woodland on the right, following the path as it parallels the road. At a cross track turn left. Cross the road and go straight onto a track, opened up by recent felling. Perhaps replanting will give pleasure to future generations.

Continue into a field, turning left to follow beside the woodland. At a track junction continue on the track ahead. A seat and a topograph give the opportunity to enjoy the view. The path rises to woodland. Pass over a stile to the road and immediately turn left into the woodland on a bridleway. This emerges into a field, giving a view of Chastleton House across to the right.

The view from Chastleton towards the vale of Moreton.

Built in the early 1600s, and little altered in succeeding centuries, it is now a National Trust property. It has undergone extensive restoration before re-opening to the public in 1996 or 1997.

At the end of the woodland, turn left. Strike half right across the field, and the next. Aim for a field corner and enter the field to follow its left-hand boundary, crossing it to follow the other side and into the next field. The path follows parallel to the right-hand boundary and then bears left across to the far left-hand corner. In the last field follow a track back to the Village Hall.

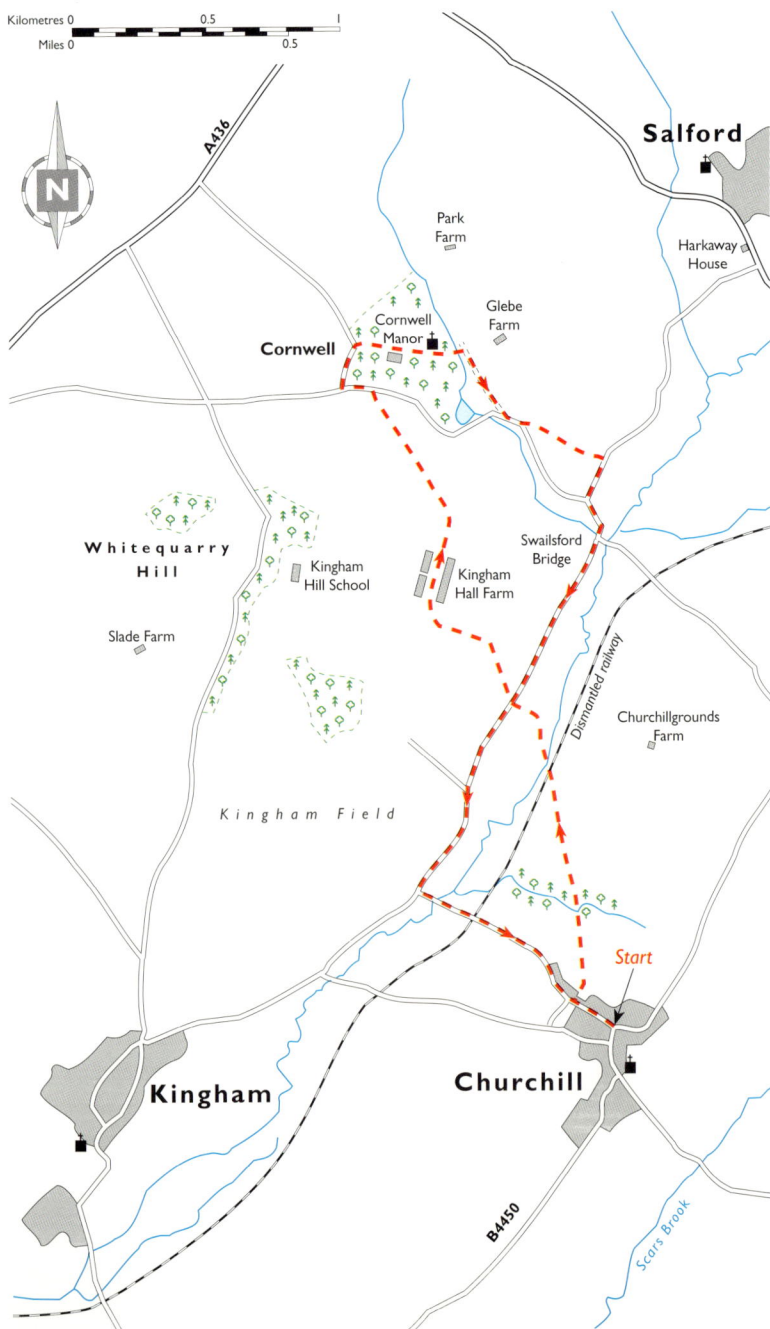

Kilometres 0   0.5   1
Miles 0   0.5

N

A436

Salford

Park Farm

Harkaway House

Cornwell

Cornwell Manor

Glebe Farm

Whitequarry Hill

Kingham Hill School

Slade Farm

Kingham Hall Farm

Swailsford Bridge

Dismantled railway

Churchillgrounds Farm

Kingham Field

Start

Kingham

Churchill

B4450

Scars Brook

CHURCHILL AND CORNWELL

Strangely, Churchill does not mean a church on a hill, but a mound or tumulus on a hill. The present church, which dominates the skyline, was only built in the 1820s as a successor to the ancient church down the hill, on this route towards the end. The 'new' church was designed with an Oxford college theme; the tower resembling that at Magdalen, and hammerbeam roof that of Christ Church. It stands starkly in an enclosure without the usual family of headstones commemorating parishioners over the centuries who have 'gone before'. They are at the old church.

INFORMATION

Distance: Full walk – 9 km (5 miles); short walk – 4 km (2 miles).

Start and finish: Church opposite The Chequers. Churchill is south-west of Chipping Norton on the B4450.

Car parking: Park discreetly. The road is wide near the start.

Terrain: Easy walking in rolling country. No special footwear needed.

Time: Full walk – allow 3 hours; short walk – allow I hour.

Refreshments: Churchill: The Chequers.

A suitably rugged stone to commemorate William Smith, "the father of British geology".

The path uses a part of the D'Arcy Dalton Way, named in gratitude to an Oxfordshire walker who worked hard to keep the rights of way open. From the footpath sign opposite The Chequers, follow the path (church on your right) bearing left across the recreation ground to the war memorial. On the left is a memorial fountain honouring James Langston, who paid for the building of the church.

At the war memorial, turn left on the road. At the junction is a stone monument commemorating William Smith (1769–1839), known as the 'father of British geology'. He pioneered work on understanding the significance of rock strata, and in 1815 published the first Geological Map of England.

Warren Hastings, born here, went on to be first Governor General of India.

Bear right down Hastings Hill, named for the birthplace, on the right, of Warren Hastings, first Governor General of India in the late 18th century. A plaque over the door is seen through the magnolias. He bought back the family house (sold by an impecunious ancestor) at Daylesford to the north-west, and is buried in the churchyard there (Walk 19). Further down is a seat, and stile into the field on the right. Beyond the gardens, slightly left, is another stile giving access to the path across the field in the same direction to the woodland ahead.

Cross this strip of woodland, a wildlife reserve. At the far side cross the next field diagonally left down the slope to the corner. Kingham Hill School is on the skyline left. Go through the hedge and bear left across the field to a footbridge, and, in the same direction, cut across the corner of the field before reaching a track, which is the line of the former railway connecting Banbury (to the right) and Kingham, and beyond to Cheltenham.

Cross the track and enter the next field, bearing right across it to a footbridge. Bear right beyond the bridge across to the far right-hand field corner. Leave the field across a footbridge and follow the right-hand hedgeline to a track.

For the short walk turn left on the track, resuming the description at the penultimate paragraph.

For the full walk, cross the track, go over a stile and bear diagonally right across the next field, to a point about midway in the hedgeline ahead. Bear left up the slope beside this hedge. At the farm drive, continue ahead and right, through the farm buildings, to a gate, and through it to a second.

Bear half left to a stile/footbridge across the hedge, and straight across the next field, to a gateway into another, and bear left up to a stile at the top. Bear half right across the parkland pasture to a roadside stile to the left of Cornwell Manor, seen on the other side of the road.

A better view of the Manor is gained through the ornamental gates beside the road. The south front is mid 18th century, but the house behind is older. In the 1930s it was restored by the architect Clough Williams-Ellis, who also landscaped the valley between the gates and the house. Perhaps his best known work is the Italianate village of Portmeirion in North Wales.

Return along the road to turn right at a crossroads (signed Moreton in Marsh), thus passing Cornwell village in the angle (the lane through the village is not a right of way). Beyond a farm, turn right to a footpath sign directing you diagonally left through an orchard. Over the stile, turn right to follow the fence, cross another stile, and go left into an avenue of trees to the churchyard.

Beyond the church, bear left to a kissing-gate and cross the pasture down the valley and up to a road. Turn right, passing Glebe Farm. At the junction, bear left and shortly left again on a bridleway into a field. Go straight across to the right-hand end of a line of trees and follow the hedge in the next field. Turn right at the road and left at the junction.

After 200 m (before reaching the road bridge), turn right onto a bridleway. Follow it for nearly a kilometre, to the point where the short walk rejoins. Walk for 500 m, to join the access road for Kingham Hill School (above right). Follow the surfaced road as it turns left. Pass by Churchill Mill, now converted to dwellings, and over the old railway at Sarsden Halt, curiously named thus when Sarsden is the other side of Churchill.

Follow the road up the hill, passing the old church on the right (only the chancel remains), and lastly, turn right towards the new church.

The remains of Churchill's "old" church with its family of gravestones.

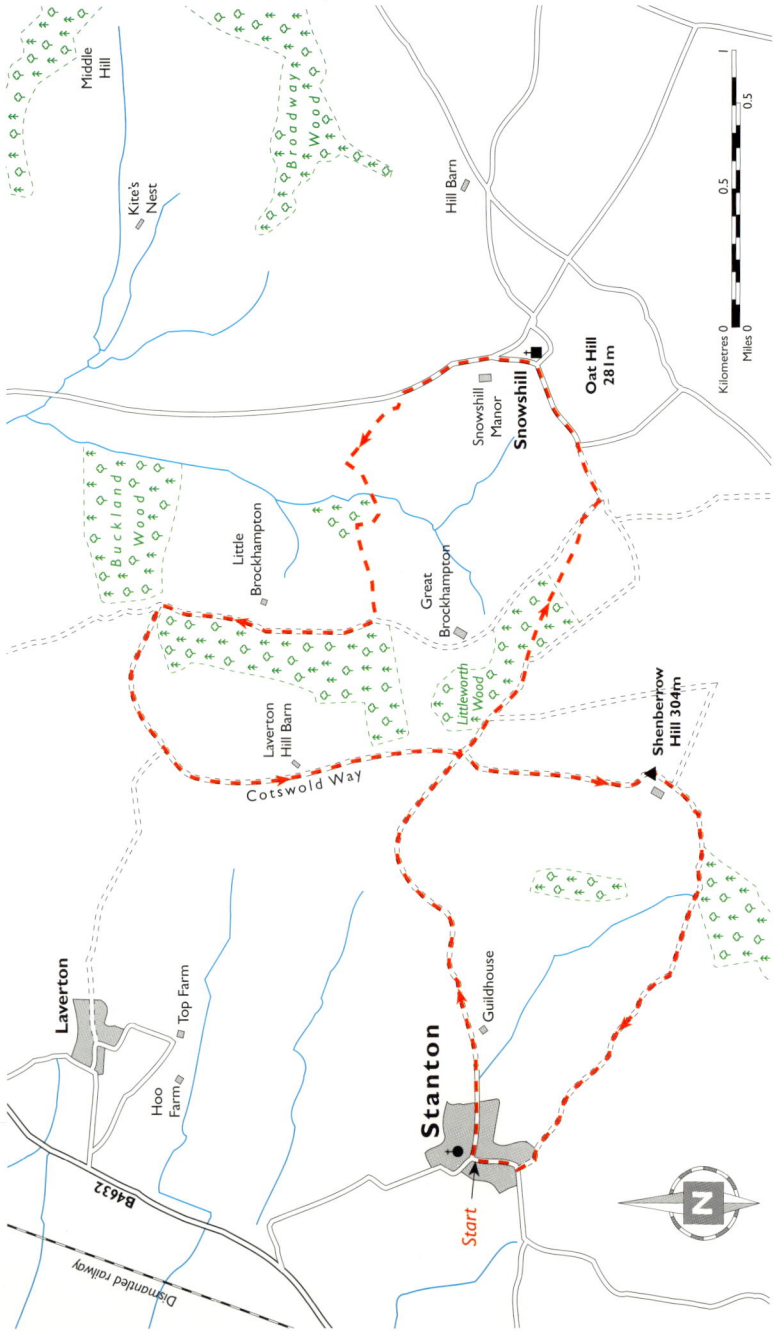

Middle
Hill

Kite's
Nest

Broadway Wood

Hill Barn

Buckland Wood

Snowshill
Manor

Snowshill

Oat Hill
281m

Little
Brockhampton

Great
Brockhampton

*Littleworth
Wood*

Laverton
Hill Barn

**Shenberrow
Hill 304m**

Cotswold Way

Laverton

Top Farm

Hoo
Farm

B4632

Dismantled railway

Guildhouse

Stanton

Start

Kilometres 0

Miles 0

0.5

0.5

N

STANTON AND SNOWSHILL

From the car park, turn right to the corner of the village street. Bear left up the hill, passing 17th century houses, built from the prosperity of the wool trade. They later fell into decay, but were rescued by Sir Philip Stott in the first quarter of the 20th century. The church, to the left beyond the village cross, has associations with John Wesley.

A typical Cotswold cottage with the village cross cross and Stanton church behind

Following the left hand, major, road, pass to the right of the Mount Inn, and left of the entrance to the Guildhouse. Turn right up the track, signed 'Public Path', onto the open hillside above. The track leads up past old quarry areas. At the top beyond a gate, the track levels and the Cotswold Way crosses it, in an area known locally as 'No Man's Land' (not true now, of course!).

Snowshill street scene.

Continue on the lane ahead. After 200 m turn left into the National Trust's Littleworth Wood. The path descends through this mixed woodland. At a junction of paths take the right-hand, upper, path to emerge shortly into a field. Bear left diagonally down to a gate. Snowshill is on the hillside opposite.

At the gate turn right to a junction. Turn left along the track passing houses, to a junction with the road. Turn left and walk into Snowshill village. Pass a wall on the left where the two parts of staddlestones have been incorporated; the square-cut vertical tapering support and the round top which resembles a mushroom when normally mounted together. Granaries were mounted on these because the horizontal underside of the top kept out rats.

The church, built in 1864, and the graveyard occupy the centre of the village. Beyond the Snowshill Arms is Snowshill Manor. Charles Paget Wade gathered an incredible collection of artefacts here from all over the world, guided by the principle that mankind's ingenuity should be marvelled at, in all its forms. Musical instruments, oriental furniture and armour, old bicycles, model farm waggons, and much more, feature in the collection. The gardens are delightful too. The 17th-century building can be glimpsed through the grill in the door, but the official entrance is now 500 m further along the road beside it.

Following this road past classic Cotswold cottages, pass the first car park on the left, reaching the modern drive and main entrance to the Manor. If visiting the Manor, return to this point afterwards, to continue the walk.

Cross the stile on the right of the drive entrance. Proceed parallel to the hedge to another stile, then diagonally left to another, incorporating an old stone stile. A notice advises the legal diversion to the bottom left corner of the steeply sloping field. The original path led to the farm on the hillside above right.

Through the gate into the woodland, the path reaches the edge and follows it around to the right, eventually emerging at a stile and climbing the open hillside beside a fence, to a kissing gate at a road. Turn right, passing the drive to Little Brockhampton. Across the valley is Broadway Tower and, a little below it to the right, Middle Hill House with its semicircular front wall.

Turning left through a gate, enjoy the view over the vales of Severn and Evesham. Bear left across the grass to two waymark posts, before descending to an old stone gatepost beside the track. Turn left on the track which carries the Cotswold Way back to 'No Man's Land', passing through woodland and fields, with Laverton Hill Barn and more old quarry workings. Cross the track, to the gate a little to the left.

Follow the Cotswold Way on the track to a path junction at the remains of the ramparts of Shenberrow iron-age hill fort. Turn left. (If you wish to see the view from the hillfort, come back to this point as the rights of way do not link up beyond.)

Follow the line of the old defences, now growing mature trees, bearing right through farm buildings. Pass the gateway to the farmhouse. Continue on the bridleway ahead (blue arrow) to follow the field edge by the woodland through two fields to a gate.

Follow the bridleway forward to the right-hand side of the woodland ahead. Bear right down the hill through four fields, aiming to the left of Stanton church spire. On the right above the village is the Stanton Guildhouse, the inspiration of Mary Osborne who gathered the resources to build it as a centre for the teaching of arts and crafts.

Stanton "stone town" though Cotswold slats gave way to Welsh blue slates when they became cheaper.

Follow the Chestnut Farm drive, bearing right to the village road. Proceed ahead, passing half-timbered barns rescued from the vale and converted to dwellings. Turn left at the road junction and back to the start.

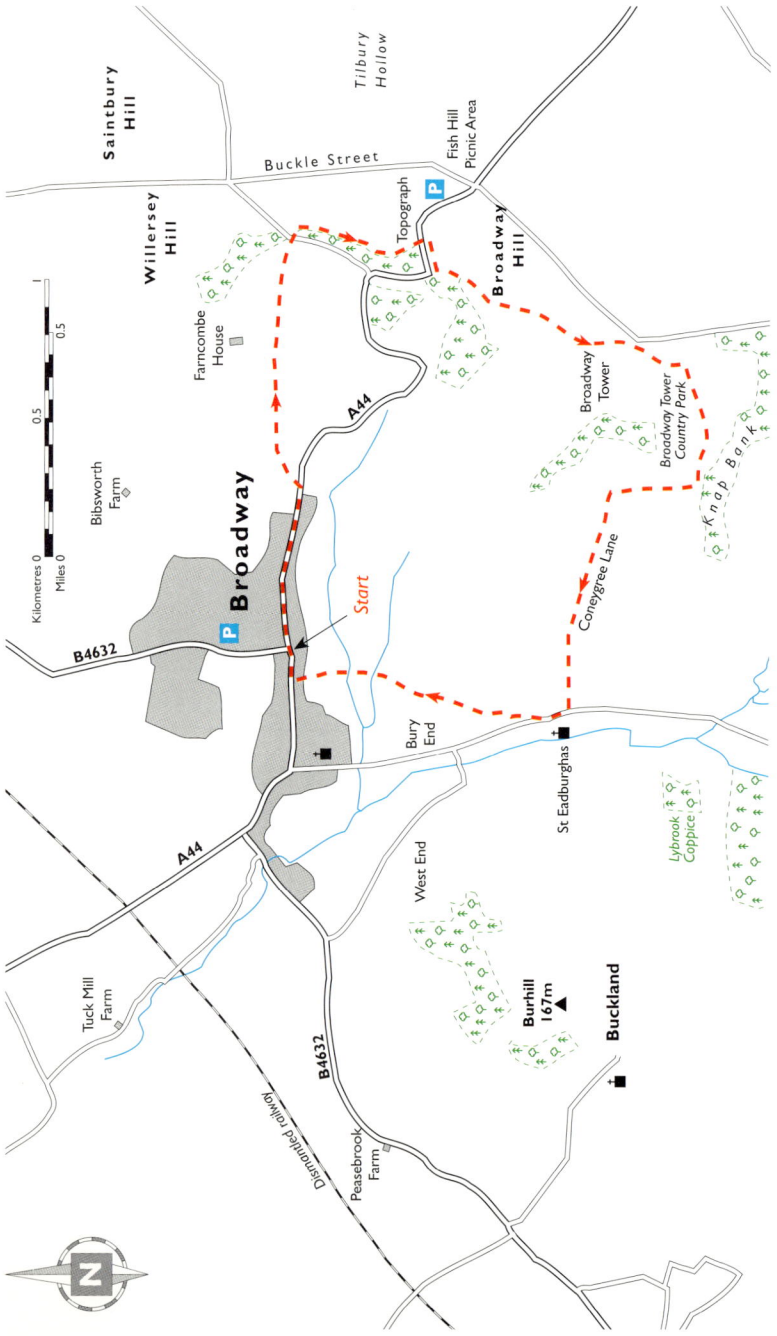

Saintbury
Hill

*Tilbury
Hollow*

Willersey
Hill

Buckle Street

Fish Hill
Picnic Area

Topograph

Broadway Hill

Farncombe
House

A44

Broadway
Tower

Broadway Tower
Country Park

Knap Bank

Bibsworth
Farm

Broadway

Start

B4632

P

Coneygree Lane

Bury
End

St Eadburghas

*Lybrook
Coppice*

West End

A44

Tuck Mill
Farm

B4632

Dismantled railway

Peasebrook
Farm

**Burhill
167m**

Buckland

Kilometres 0
Miles 0
0.5
0.5
1

BROADWAY

Broadway rightly welcomes thousands of visitors a year. Early mornings and late evenings in summer are the best times to enjoy the feast of buildings along the main street. Overlooking the Green at the lower end is a delightful mixture of half-timbering and stone in the Broadway Hotel. Opposite is Wisteria Cottage, which is indeed swathed in wisteria, and smothered in blossom in season.

Further up is the Lygon Arms, previously the White Hart. General Lygon fought at Waterloo and his estate was at Springhill, on the hills above, where it is said he laid out plantations in the formation of the armies at the battle. The hotel was taken over by the Russells in the early 20th century. On the land behind, Sir Gordon Russell developed an internationally renowned furniture business.

Unlike some, he recognised the value of mass produced articles in maintaining cash flow to support the more prestigious products. When radio spread rapidly in the 1930s, many of the bodies for the sets were made here. Near the bus stop is the shop of S&D Jelfs, made up of two cottages - one roofed in Cotswold slate, the other in recently renewed thatch.

From the Leamington Road junction, the route follows the left side of the main street up the hill. The buildings, from ancient cottages to the Victorian police station, provide continuous interest. On the right is a development of cottages from the old Coach and Horses Inn, which can be identified by the inn signpost (minus board). Towards the top are old farmhouses converted into residences. Beyond the last house (Pike Cottage) bear left into a field. Follow iron railings on the left.

After stile and gate, follow the right-hand boundary, the track becoming sunken and stony. In the next field, follow the left-hand boundary, then across up to a stile. Bearing slightly right, the path reaches a road at the entrance to the Group 4 establishment.

INFORMATION

Distance: 8 km (5 miles).

Start and finish: (a) Broadway main street, or (b) Fish Hill Picnic Area.

Car parking: (a) Broadway: Leamington Road – pay and display. From the parking area walk back to the road, turn left to reach main street. (b) Fish Hill Picnic Area (no charge). Walk up to the topograph and join the walk there. Remember the climb is at the end of the walk!

Public transport: Castleways buses from Evesham and Cheltenham, and other operators from Evesham. Alight in main street near the Lygon Arms (return from stop outside S&D Jelfs). Walk up the street to the Leamington Road junction.

Terrain: One climb, otherwise ridge and field walking. Boots or strong shoes recommended.

Time: Allow 3–4 hours.

Refreshments: Broadway: Inns and cafés. Broadway Tower.

Toilets: Broadway: Car parks. Fish Hill Picnic Area.

Opening hours: *Broadway Tower:* 1 Apr- 31 Oct, 1000–1800.

Half-right across the road junction, cross the stile; turn left to follow a stepped slope. Turn right below a large barn. Keep to the upper path through the woodland - largely beech with many saplings ready to succeed the mature specimens. Ignore right-hand paths and red arrows.

Turn left and down a stepped path. Further on, climb steps on the left and turn right to follow the path, close to the left-hand field, into the Fish Hill Picnic Area. Walk up to the topograph. Those parking at Fish Hill Picnic Area walk up the steps to join the walk here. The topograph, carved with a map centred on the site, shows distances to many local and faraway places, but the only view is to the north, towards the outlier of Meon Hill and the Warwickshire plain.

Down the steep bank below the topograph (opposite the steps) turn left and right to follow the Cotswold Way down to the A44 road. Cross with care to a waymark post on the other side. Rise to a quarry track, immediately turning right into the woodland. Bear left to a wider track and turn left towards a gate/stile leading out to open fields.

Broadway Tower.

Waymark posts guide you across the hillocks and valleys until the main 'waymark' comes into view - the turrets of Broadway Tower. The field before the Tower is the part of the National Trust's Clump Farm. The valley is formed by the hillside 'peeling' away from the main mass over many centuries.

Go through the gates into Broadway Tower Country Park. An admission charge is payable except for those who keep to the public footpath. The formidable gates and fences are for keeping the deer enclosed.

The Tower houses exhibitions about its history and connections with the Earl of Coventry, Sir Thomas Phillips of book collecting fame and its use as a 'holiday cottage' by Pre-Raphaelite artists such as William Morris, whose letter from here prompted the founding of the Society for the Preservation of

Ancient Buildings. It was a farmhouse until conversion for the country park.

The public footpath follows the ridge, through a group of four trees, to another deer gate and the entry kiosk for the Park. Turn right, explain if necessary that you are walking the public footpath, and pass to the right of the Rookery Barn, transplanted from the farm below. You may enter the barn for refreshment without paying for admission, but if you stray further the charge is payable.

A mixture of architecture and a cottage garden in Broadway.

The waymarked path by the fence leads over a ladder stile to another gate/stile. Beyond this, turn right down the road. Where it turns left, bear right on the track below the houses. At the gate, turn right onto a track which passes cottages on the right, and presents a view over Broadway and the vales of Evesham and Severn towards the Clee Hills, 80 km north-west in Shropshire.

Beyond the gate/stile a leafy track turns sharp left down Coneygree Lane, a major route up the scarp centuries ago but now quiet mixed woodland. In summer the sounds of cricket may be heard to the left before reaching the lodge house and the road.

Turn right. Immediately on the left is St Eadburgha's church, which served Broadway until St Michael's was built closer to the present settlement. Services are still held in summer, and lighting is by candles.

Along the road from the church, pass The Court on the left. Beyond farm buildings on the right the footpath enters the field to follow the right-hand hedge. Continue beyond, beside an embankment. Over the stile, follow another embankment on the left marking the line of an old hedge. In the next field follow the old hedge. The path crosses the old ridge and furrow of the open field system before the Enclosures.

Crossing the stream, walk straight ahead to the corner of the next field. Beyond the stile, walk between the apple and pear trees beside a recreation ground. The narrow path by a high garden wall leads into the main street of Broadway. Turn left for the main shopping area (and the bus) and right to Leamington Road.

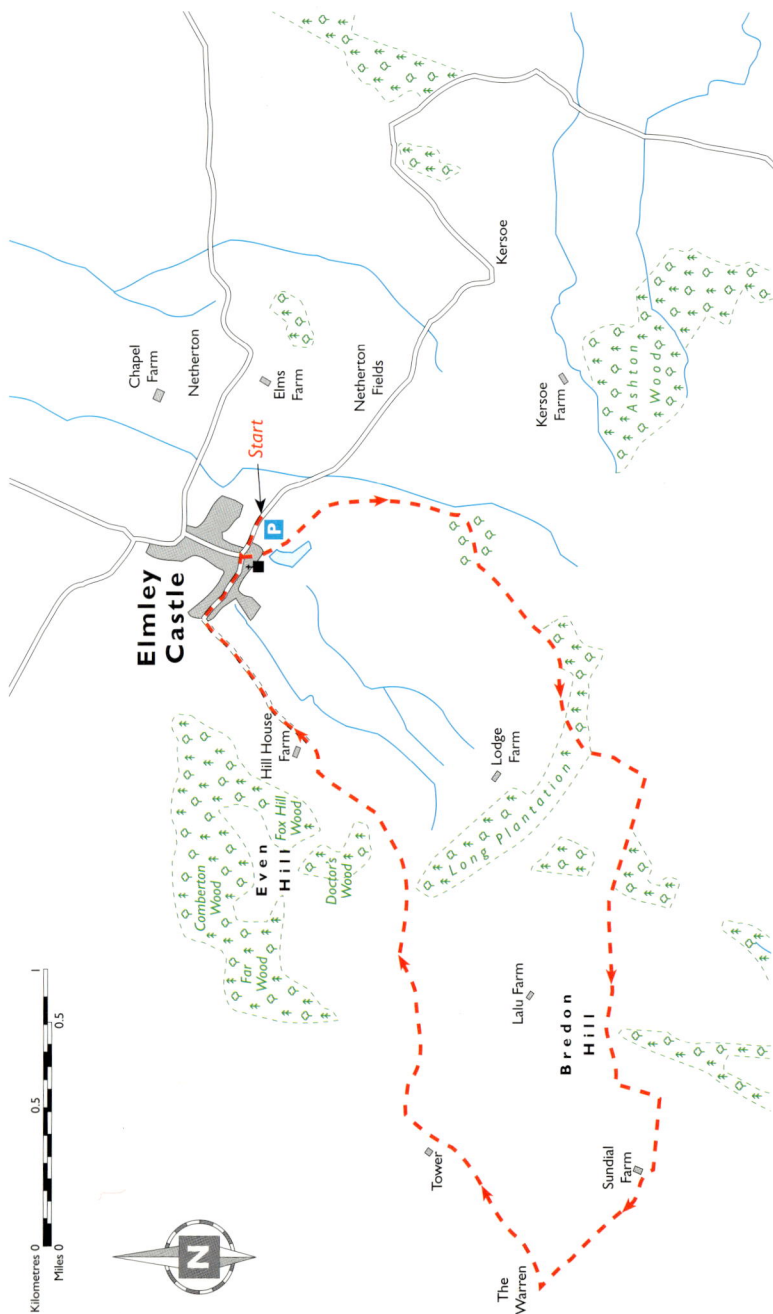

Chapel
Farm
Netherton

Elms
Farm

Netherton
Fields

Kersoe

Ashton Wood

Kersoe
Farm

Start

P

Elmley
Castle

Hill House
Farm

Lodge
Farm

Comberton
Wood

Even
Hill

Fox Hill
Wood

Doctor's
Wood

Long Plantation

Far
Wood

Lalu Farm

Bredon
Hill

Tower

Sundial
Farm

The
Warren

Kilometres 0
Miles 0

0.5

0.5

1

ELMLEY CASTLE AND BREDON HILL

Bredon Hill is a Cotswold island in the Vale; an outlier of the main Cotswold massif with similar underlying rock. However, on this borderline is a pleasing mix between Cotswold stone and Vale red brick and half-timbering. The hill is famous for its literary associations with A. E. Housman's poem in *A Shropshire Lad* and with John Moore's *Brensham Village*.

From the picnic area turn left on the road, with the playing field on your right. Emerge into Elmley Castle's main street from a narrow passage between houses, opposite the Queen Elizabeth Inn, and turn left. Walk into the churchyard. An interesting sundial tells the time and a note in the church porch not only relates its history but tells how Elmley sun time is slow on Greenwich.

Elmley Castle's unusual sundial.

The path leaves the churchyard to the left of the church, passing over the outflow of a small lake, and crosses two stiles. The path strictly goes across the field, bearing right in the middle. It is probably better to take the route round the right-hand edge, indicated with a white marker. After turning the corners, turn right over a footbridge and stile. Bear left to the far left corner. The hill on the right was topped at one time with a castle (which gave the village its name) but it was already in ruins in the 14th century. A deer park surrounds it.

Over the stile on the left, turn right through a bridlegate, and join the Wychavon Way, which starts

at the River Severn north of Droitwich, ending 65 km south in Winchcombe. It was created to celebrate the Queen's Silver Jubilee in 1977, and symbolically unite Droitwich, Pershore and Evesham after local government re-organisation created Wychavon District.

Turn right to follow a track between the woodlands of Ailes Grove on the right and Fiddler's Knap on the left. Crossing the small stream, bear left to climb the hill. The field narrows to a bridlegate. Take a moment to pause while closing it behind you to enjoy the view over the Vale of Evesham, flanked on the right by another Cotswold outlier, Meon Hill.

Follow the path up through the woodland, finally walking beside high fencing which keeps out deer. At the top, in the open, the Wychavon Way leaves on the left. Cross to the bridleway through the gates almost opposite. Follow the headland by the wall. After two fields, turn right beside crop fields and woodlands. A radio mast is on the right. Continue ahead on its access road to the next junction. Continue ahead over Bredon Hill to a track.

Turn left and then next right to Sundial Farm. The dwelling is ruined but one barn is retained, complete

The remaining barn at Sundial Farm.

with sundial and unusual entry door. The track continues but before leaving the farm enclosure, turn right over a stile to follow a headland path to the belt of trees ahead. Turn right into this woodland and in the next field the tower of Parson's Folly appears, and is reached after passing through the ramparts of the Iron Age hill fort.

The tower was built to bring the height of the hill up to 1000 feet (310 m). Now used for mounting radio transmitting equipment on its walls, it is easy to see why. The view from Broadway Tower in the east, southwards round to Birmingham in the north, makes a full, unobstructed three-quarter circle.

In the dip beside the tower is the Banbury Stone, an 'erratic' or stone of different composition; the reason for its presence unexplained. Smaller stones here are sometimes arranged in patterns on the grass with no more antiquity than the whim of present day visitors.

Follow the wall round the scarp edge (ignore a gate in it), and pass by the end of the hill fort ramparts again, leaving the field at a gate to the left of a copse. The path now generally follows the edge, curving round to the right. It may not be wholly clear on the ground, but it is a bridleway and the writer found some particularly equine waymarks quite a useful guide! It finally descends to the left of woodland, crossing another bridleway called Double Hedges Road connecting the north side of the hill to the south.

Follow the fence line on the right. There is a fine view of the deer park of Elmley Castle. Continuing with the fence on the right, through a gate into rough pasture, aim for a junction of tracks below. Take the narrow track with a fence on the left, entering a sunken track through the trees. At the half-timbered Hill House Farm the track becomes a road. Follow it past several half-timbered black and white houses all the way back to the Queen Elizabeth Inn and the main street.

Half timbered cottages are a feature of Elmley Castle.

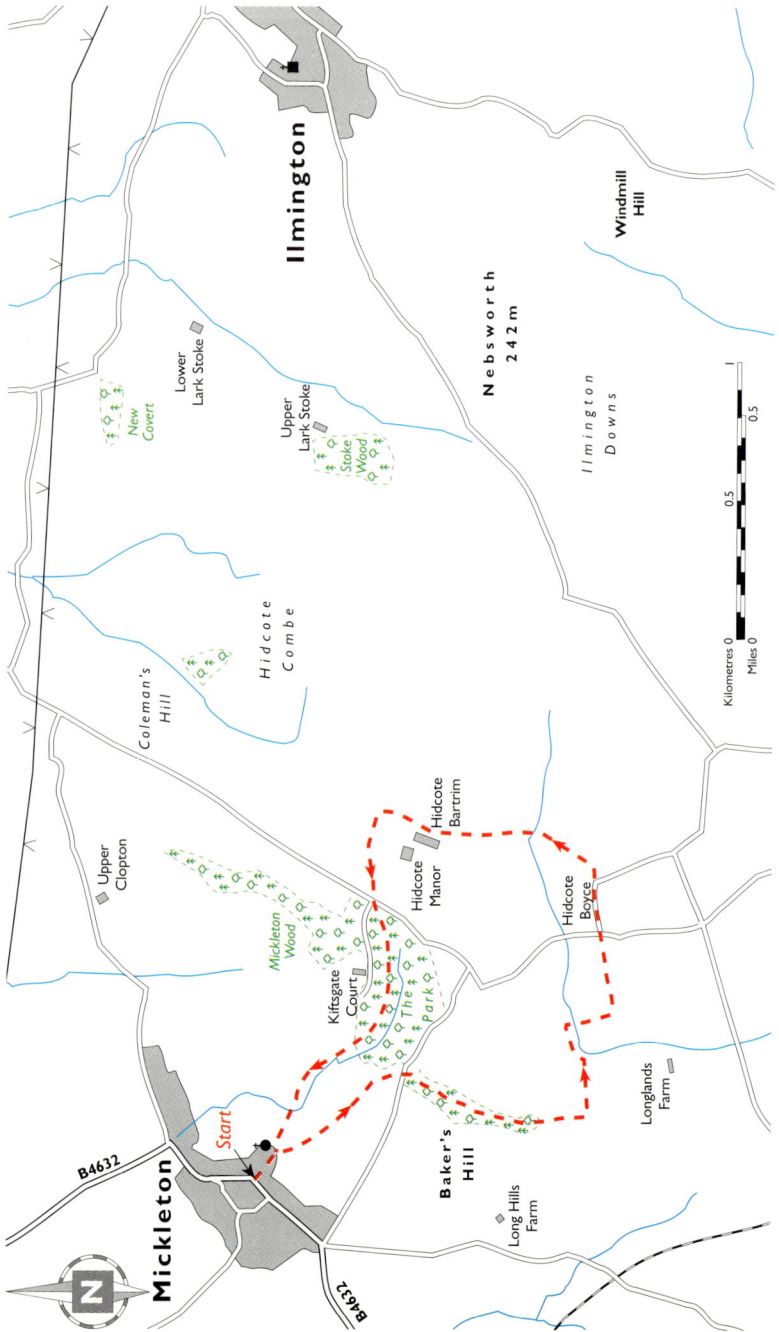

Ilmington

Windmill
Hill

Nebsworth
242 m

Ilmington Downs

Lower
Lark Stoke

New
Covert

Upper
Lark Stoke

Stoke
Wood

Hidcote
Combe

Coleman's
Hill

Kilometres 0
Miles 0

0.5

0.5

Upper
Clopton

Hidcote
Bartrim

Mickleton
Wood

Hidcote
Manor

Hidcote
Boyce

Kiftsgate
Court

The
Park

Start

Longlands
Farm

B4632

Mickleton

Baker's
Hill

Long Hills
Farm

B4632

MICKLETON AND HIDCOTE

This is a shorter walk with the opportunity to visit two famous gardens. From the telephone box walk away from the main road towards the church of St Lawrence. Originally founded in the 12th century and since expanded, it was restored in the 1860s. There are several 'hatchments', boards with heraldic symbols representing local families, which were used at funerals. After visiting the church resume the walk on the lane as it bears left. Turn right onto a footpath to the right of the cemetery. In the field keep to the right-hand side and descend to a stile, giving access to a strip of woodland.

At the far end, enter a field and keep to the left-hand edge as far as a gate. Turn half-right to follow a line of trees rising to the road. Across the road ascend the steps to a stile, and turn right in the field. This is part of the Heart of England Way (southbound here) which was devised by a dedicated group of volunteers before official recognition. It connects Cannock Chase in Staffordshire with Bourton on the Water in Gloucestershire.

After following the field edge for 200 m, the path enters the woodlands of Baker's Hill. These are mature, if not over-mature, beech woodlands, some trees having survived the attentions of graffiti writers. Views to the vale below are obviously better in winter.

Enter a rough field, followed by another cultivated field, and reach a barn. Turn left to the road. Leaving

INFORMATION

Distance: 6 km (4 miles).

Start and finish: Telephone box at road junction by Manor. Mickleton is on the B4632 between Stratford on Avon and Broadway.

Car parking: Some parking spaces at the start. Otherwise park discreetly in the village.

Public transport: Midland Red South/ Stratford Blue from Stratford. Other services on certain days by other operators.

Terrain: Gentle ascent and descent of scarp through field and woodland.

Time: Allow 3 hours.

Refreshments: Mickleton: Kings Arms, Butchers Arms, Three Ways Hotel. Hidcote Bartrim: Hidcote Manor Gardens on garden open days.

Opening hours: *Hidcote Manor Gardens (National Trust):* Apr–end Oct, daily except Tue and Fri, 1100–1900. Admission charge. *Kiftsgate Court Gardens:* 1 Apr–30 Sep, Sun, Wed and Thu plus Bank Holiday Mondays, plus Sat in Jun and Jul, 1400–1800. Admission charge.

The open wold near Hidcote Boyce.

the Heart of England Way, turn left again on the road for a few metres, in order to bear right to follow the left-hand hedgeline in the field. The village of Hidcote Boyce appears ahead.

Cross a footbridge into the next field and follow the left-hand hedgeline again. Hidcote House now appears ahead. Turn right along the southbound hedgeline, and turn left at a gate (stile beside). Follow the right-hand side of this broad avenue, recently planted, and into an enclosed path to the road.

Cross the road and follow the lane straight ahead, up through Hidcote Boyce. A row of staddlestones can be examined at eye level on a wall on the right. Originally, granaries were mounted on staddlestones to keep out vermin. Rats could not negotiate the horizontal underside of the mushroom-like top.

Ignore two roads on the right. Beyond Top Farm, bear half left across the field and pass through the hedge into the next field. Bear slightly left up the rise towards a large mid-field tree and the chimney pots of Hidcote Bartrim. The upper part of the field is devoted to 'pick your own' soft fruit. Continue past a barn and into the lane fronted with classic Cotswold cottages to reach Hidcote Manor.

The Manor itself is not open but the attraction is the work started by Major Lawrence Johnston, an American, who created the gardens from 1905 onwards. It is a mixture of small intimate gardens and long vistas; of a profusion of plants tumbling informally in a small valley, and of formally clipped trees and hedges; of displays of old roses and much, much more besides. The Theatre Lawn hosts open-air performances in early July.

The walk passes the gates of the Gardens and proceeds to a junction with the access road. Note the avenue ahead. This used to be a magnificent line of tall mature elms arching over to touch each other, presenting the aspect of the nave of a great cathedral. Completely devastated in the late 1970s by Dutch Elm disease, it has been replanted with other species, although you can still find shrubby elm nearby.

Turn left down the access road to the junction; Kiftsgate Court Garden entrance is on the right. This is another opportunity to indulge yourself in magnificent gardens, this time created by three generations of ladies – Mrs Muir, Mrs Binny and Mrs Chambers. As at Hidcote, the house is not open, but is used to great effect as the garden backdrop.

When the original manor house in Mickleton was dismantled at the end of the 19th century, some of the façades were incorporated here. Heather Muir, who started the garden around 1920, was a friend of Lawrence Johnston's at Hidcote Manor, and no doubt this would have benefitted both gardens.

The return to Mickleton is through the gate immediately opposite the Hidcote lane, and to the left of the Kiftsgate entrance. However, it is not immediately obvious because it is set at right angles to the road, between two offset walls. With the tree-lined scarp and gardens of Kiftsgate rising above you on the right, walk down the valley to gates between woodland. Then maintain the same height across the next pasture before gently descending to a bridlegate to the right of the bottom of the field.

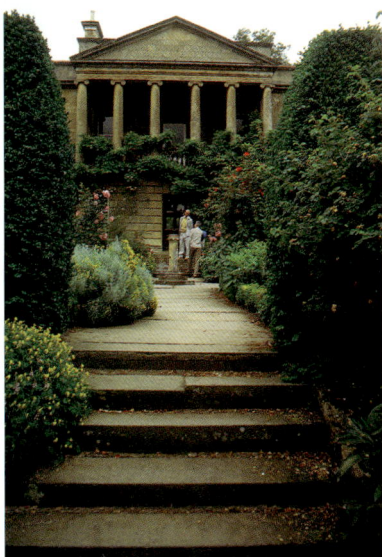

Kiftsgate Gardens.

In the next field, follow the boundary round to the left; ignore the footpath going left and continue through the bridlegate ahead. As you keep to the left-hand hedgeline, Meon Hill, the most northerly Cotswold outlier, can be seen to the right. This path is on the Heart of England Way again, but this time northbound.

Through another gate, the path leads you across the field, to turn left beyond the cemetery wall and back into the lane to the start.

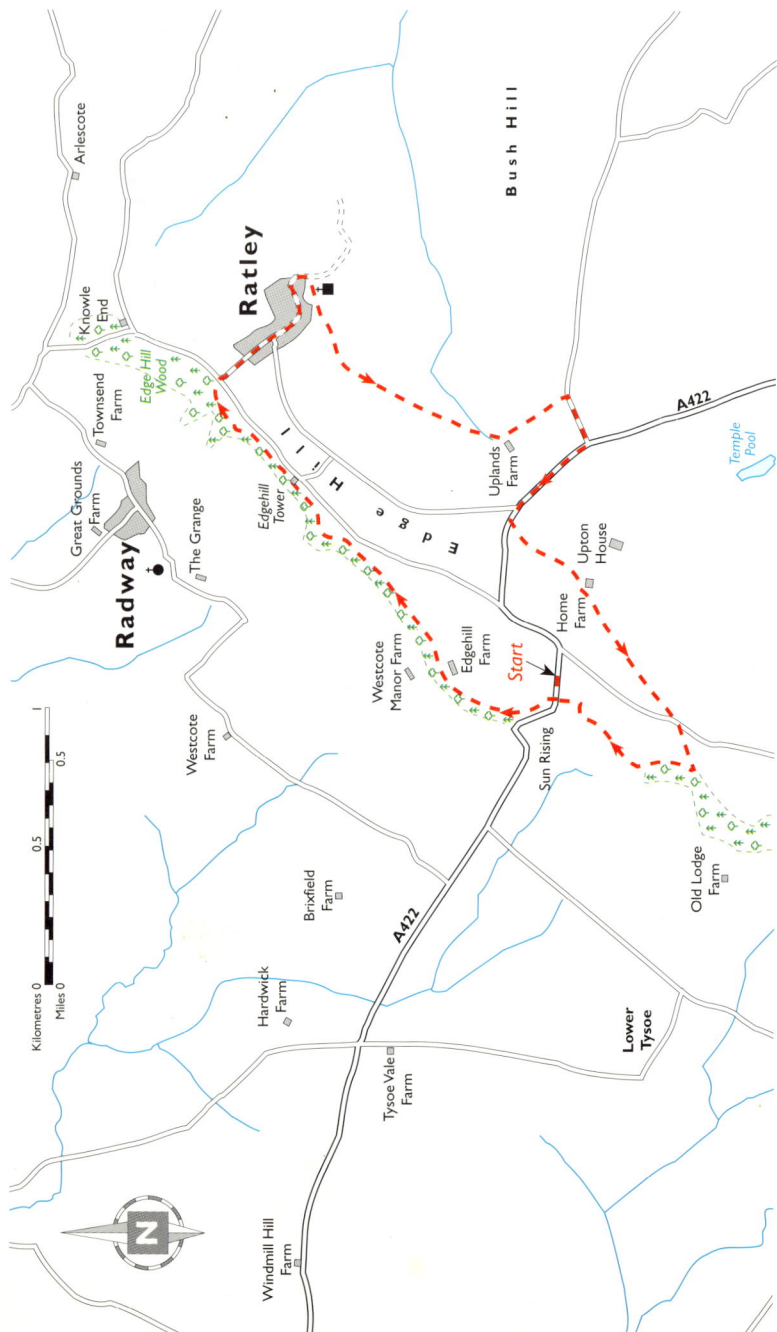

Arlescote

Bush Hill

Knowle End

Ratley

Townsend Farm

Edge Hill Wood

Great Grounds Farm

Radway

The Grange

Edgehill Tower

E d g e   H i l l

Uplands Farm

A422

Temple Pool

Upton House

Home Farm

Start

Westcote Manor Farm

Edgehill Farm

Sun Rising

Westcote Farm

Old Lodge Farm

Brixfield Farm

A422

Hardwick Farm

Lower Tysoe

Tysoe Vale Farm

Windmill Hill Farm

Kilometres 0
Miles 0
0.5
0.5

N

EDGE HILL
AND UPTON HOUSE

Edge Hill, one of twin 'promontories' pointing north into Warwickshire, marks the northern extremity of the Cotswolds, over 110 km from the most southern point. The stone is darker, showing the presence of iron.

Viewed from a distance, Edge Hill looks like a scarp edge topped by a plateau. In fact, a valley system runs south from Ratley, protected by the rim of the northern scarp. The Civil War's opening battle, which was indecisive, took place on the plain below the hill on 23 October 1642. King Charles I is said to have raised his banner on the site of the 18th-century Castle Hotel.

Starting from the lay-by at the top of Sun Rising Hill, walk down the hill on the right-hand verge. Before reaching Sun Rising House, note a drive on the other side of the road. On your side a path leads into the woodland. Turn right and follow it as it weaves its way towards the scarp edge. The route is waymarked as part of the Centenary Way, created by Warwickshire County Council to mark its hundredth birthday in 1989. It runs from north Warwickshire to Ilmington on the other northern promontory of the Cotswolds.

The scarp is wooded and contains many fine mature trees, among them oak, beech and horse chestnut. Their successors are struggling beneath the canopy but

The Warwickshire Feldon and the village of Radway.

one day their turn will come. Occasional gaps give a view out to the Warwickshire Feldon or field lands (contrasting with Arden and its one-time forest to the north). The village below is Radway, and the Grange mansion can be seen, where Henry Fielding wrote part of *Tom Jones*.

Ratley village at the head of the valley behind the scarp edge.

Below Edge Hill Farm, turn left down the road a short distance before resuming the Way on the right. Along this section, Cotswold Voluntary Wardens have been revetting the path and building steps, some with handrails. Follow their work if the waymarking is not clear.

Join the sunken bridleway of King John's Lane for a few metres and leave it again by bearing right to keep height. At a cross-path junction climb the handrailed slope to the right for the Castle Hotel. The Way turns left at the top on a bridleway. If you do not wish to climb, take the level footpath which converges on the same bridleway further on. Turn right and ascend Jacob's Ladder with its 83 steps, in sections, to bring you to the road.

Cross over and follow the road signposted 'Ratley only'. Take the upper (left-hand) fork to pass the village hall and, further down, the chapel which gives the lane its name. At the bottom is a small green with the Rose and Crown Inn to the left and the church to the right.

Turn right past the church; the road presents a view of the valley. At the open space, instead of bearing right to ascend the hill, turn left to a gate labelled Manor Farm. Passing through two more gates, bear right following below the embankment of the ancient 'motte and baileys' marked on maps.

In the field beyond, climb half-left, converging on the skyline hedge to reach two stiles near a metal barn. Cross the left-hand stile, immediately turning right to follow the right-hand hedgeline through two fields. The second is very large and contains ruined farm buildings.

Beyond the gate, the path enters rougher ground which rises to Uplands Farm. Turn left along the fence. Follow the path behind a barn, and emerge into a field. Follow the left-hand edge, turn right at the road, and right again at the junction, taking care along 500 m of busy road, to reach Upton House on the left.

Upton House, built in the late 17th century, has a fine garden and is noted for collections of porcelain, tapestries, furniture and paintings. Beyond the entrance, turn left and bear right into a field. Walk across to converge on the fence on the right which conducts you to another gate. Half right brings you to the corner of Home Farm and its horse-exercising area. Turn left beside it to strike up the bank to a stile. Bear slightly right, straight across the next two fields to a road.

Cross the road and, through the gate, bear half left across the field. At the woodland, turn sharp right onto the track, again carrying the Centenary Way. Go quietly; you may see deer. The next field gives views far into Warwickshire, Worcestershire and beyond towards Birmingham and the north-west.

The valley below is called the Vale of Red Horse because a horse was at one time cut into the hillside in a similar way to the chalk figures on the Wessex Downs, but not so long ago; the different colour is due to different geology.

Continue along the bank, into more recently planted woodland. Turn right, then left onto the track bringing you back to Sun Rising Hill, and a right turn back to the lay-by.

Edge Hill's tower (now a hotel) built where Charles I raised his standard before the battle.

INDEX

Opposite: Huntingdon Elms, Hidcote Manor.

Other titles in this series

25 Walks – In and Around Aberdeen
25 Walks – Deeside
25 Walks – Dumfries and Galloway
25 Walks – Edinburgh and Lothian
25 Walks – Fife
25 Walks – In and Around Glasgow
25 Walks – Highland Perthshire
25 Walks – The Scottish Borders
25 Walks – The Trossachs
25 Walks – The Western Isles
25 Walks – The Yorkshire Dales

Other titles in preparation

25 Walks – Argyll
25 Walks – In and Around Belfast
25 Walks – The Chilterns
25 Walks – Fermanagh

Long distance guides published by The Stationery Office

The West Highland Way – Official Guide
The Southern Upland Way – Official Guide

Printed in Scotland for The Stationery Office by CC. No. 70343 50C 5/96

The Stationery Office

Published by The Stationery Office and available from:

The Stationery Office Bookshops
71 Lothian Road, Edinburgh EH3 9AZ
(counter service only)
South Gyle Crescent, Edinburgh EH12 9EB
(mail, fax and telephone orders only)
0131-479 3141 Fax 0131-479 3142
49 High Holborn, London WC1V 6HB
(counter service and fax orders only)
Fax 0171-831 1326
68-69 Bull Street, Birmingham B4 6AD
0121-236 9696 Fax 0121-236 9699
33 Wine Street, Bristol BS1 2BQ
0117-926 4306 Fax 0117-929 4515
9-21 Princess Street, Manchester M60 8AS
0161-834 7201 Fax 0161-833 0634
16 Arthur Street, Belfast BT1 4GD
01232 238451 Fax 01232 235401
The Stationery Office Oriel Bookshop
The Friary, Cardiff CF1 4AA
01222 395548 Fax 01222 384347

The Stationery Office publications are also available from:

The Publications Centre
(mail, telephone and fax orders only)
PO Box 276, London SW8 5DT
General enquiries 0171-873 0011
Telephone orders 0171-873 9090
Fax orders 0171-873 8200

Accredited Agents
(see Yellow Pages)

and through good booksellers